THE POWER OF AUTHENTIC HARMONY

Magical Conversations That Transform Our World

Dr Pauline Crawford

ROSALES MAVERICKS PUBLISHING STUDIO

Las Vegas | New York | México

First published in January 2019 as Magical Conversations – Turning Conflict into Collaboration. This edition incorporates the impact of world changes brought about by the pandemic and addresses the rise of women to a harmonious and equitable status – with men - and beyond gender equality. This book starts a series called The Power of Authentic Harmony to journey towards a new landscape for women and men to thrive together in health, prosperity, and happiness.

Title: The Power of Authentic Harmony

Subtitle: Magical Conversations That Transform Our World Dr. Pauline Crawford

ISBN: 978-1-959471-01-1 (Hardback)
ISBN: 978-1-959471-05-9 (Paperback)
ISBN: 978-1-959471-06-6 (E-Book)
ISBN: 978-1-959471-10-3 (Audio Book)

Library of Congress Control Number: 2022921511

Cover design by Adriana Rosales

Edited by:

Printed in the United States of America

Publisher
RMPS, Rosales Mavericks Publishing Studio™
1180 N. Town Center Suite #100
Las Vegas, Nevada 89144
www.Adriana.Company

VISION

My legacy vision is that *Corporate Heart International* is the primary, most effective and most engaging resource to shine a positive light on the *heart* of business – the *people* – and create *harmonious* work cultures to be the most valuable contribution to health and prosperity for humanity. As men and women value **THE POWER OF AUTHENTIC HARMONY**, life enhancing activities inspire individuals, groups, and communities to communicate effectively, converse effortlessly, and work energetically from both emotions and logic combined. This is achieved in a real synergy of women and men, loving one another regardless of culture, age, experience, formal education, ethnicity, gender, and sexual identity.

Dr Pauline Crawford

Chief Vision Officer, Corporate Heart International,

Mission

"Authentic Harmony between men and women and among all diverse factions is essential if we are to resolve the collective issues we face in today's world" – Dr Pauline Crawford

My mission is to enable men and women to live, love and work in ways that expand their individual and shared creative output, especially as changes occur around them and potential conflicts arise. The objective is to convert destructive conflict into healthy collaboration thereby resolving issues in the boardroom, bedroom, classroom and/or communication in general and allowing authentic harmony to rise naturally to enhance people and prosperity …and our planet!

The intended outcome impacts every aspect of our life development, such as creating deeper friendships, ensuring long term intimate relationships, building happier families, developing team synergy and seeding enthusiastic collaboration in a personal and professional community that adds an equitable return to the bottom line.

If we are to reach these outcomes, we need new rules to replace the tired old arguments that stem from disharmony and conflict. We need to evolve together, forming agreed upon shared purpose and principles of love, trust, and respect. With genuine heartfelt meaning, these need to be driven by positive loving values and, more importantly, they should feed a core belief in human nature to share kindly and inclusively. This is about you transforming your whole life.

As we set out to agree on mutual benefits, are we each able to listen without judgment, without anger and without endeavoring to control others and/or outcomes? We can only *influence* others. We cannot change them. My objectives include helping people to share experiences, create open-minded conversations, set intentions for magical outcomes, and accord permission for all participants to contribute in a safe, welcoming, healing, harmonious space.

As we continue, let's create a mix of love, happiness, consciousness, mindfulness ... and some playfulness ... and let these elements form our guiding insight. In this manner, we can learn to listen, honor, and respect one another. When we engage with joy, curiosity, freedom of expression and a wonderment of diverse views, our relationships will grow stronger, deeper, and more sustainable. Wisdom does not arrive automatically with age, yet if the lessons taught by life's ups and downs are learned well, the ensuing wisdom will add credence to *why we are who we are* as we share our lives together.

Given this opportunity to republish my original text, Magical Conversations, I present to you *The Power of Authentic Harmony* as a collective overarching vision for all of humanity to hold sacred if we are to resolve the challenges of today. A top priority regards how women are stepping forward and voicing "STOP" to being marginalized, abused, threatened, or demeaned. Harmony only happens together. Key to this future is for women to invite men to a new landscape that embraces all from a women-centric perspective. Men need to be to be advocates as well as colleagues and companions for women if we are to achieve this shift to a new way.

At least 1 in 3 women, in the world, are abused physically and sexually. Undisclosed cases mean this is a low estimate. Inequalities such as this have been officially in the public domain since the early 1900s when women battled for equality, for the vote, for human rights, for equal pay and for authentic recognition in the business world and society as equal and different. In many countries women still have no rights, or highly limited rights. Even in supposed civilized nations, women are often perceived as second-class citizens. As half of the world population, women are the largest marginalized group anywhere in the globe.

It's time to embrace *The Power of Authentic Harmony* for women to be loved, honored, respected, and valued - *and* for women to invite men into a new landscape designed through a women-centric lens for inclusion as major partners for economic and social sustainability in business, family life and community. The destiny that I propose is a shared *Joint Custody World.* As the world has changed since January 2020, in ways we never imagined due to a pandemic that locked the world down for 2 years and is an ongoing threat in our lives, I have added my experiences into the flow of this book. The original text is expanded appropriately to ensure you, the reader, gain the knowledge and experience you need to create a life where *The Power of Authentic Harmony* is the experience of a better, more prosperous, healthy life.

DEDICATION

In my life I have been blessed with many who have a profound and lasting influence on me. The most precious influences were my mother Muriel, and my father Edward. Their selfless love and gentle guidance allowed me the freedom to choose my direction in life ... to choose the path I would follow. I remember them saying to me, more than once, that what they wanted more than anything was my happiness. When I need their gentle counsel, I hear them whisper from heaven "take responsibility for your own life and serve others as you would serve yourself – with unconditional love"

Thank you ... I vow to do my best every day to uphold this guidance.

PROLOGUE

Our world has changed and so have we. With many health, societal and economic hardships being endured across our globe as we suffer from many natural disasters, wars and political unrest and the ongoing pandemic threat, there is an ever-urgent need for ***The Power of Authentic Harmony*** among women and men to lead for a ***Joint Custody World***. If we are to be free to be ourselves and grow in healthy prosperity and wisdom, the solution cannot come from one party's perspective.

As we enter this new era - never to return to the past - let's take time to observe our journey. The pandemic, lockdown, covid virus and lockdown, working from home, entering an online world to connect us, and continuing changes in our economic and social constructs have caused even more CHAOS than ever imagined. Listening to a global tribe of men and women in monthly Wisdom Circles - gatherings over Zoom through 2020-2021 - has given me a pandora's box of insights that need to be shared. This book emerges from *my* life story *and* everyone who I have met over my journey of discovery. Through theirs and my real-life experiences, I identified and developed heart-centered values and principles, a way to understand men and women, designed archetypes and a map to help me navigate my way, and endeavored to keep an open mind about our different perspectives on life in search of *The Power of Authentic Harmony.*

Given what I have learned during my journey to date, I invite *you:*

- to observe yourself, know yourself and the people around you,
- to engage others in conversations and relationships that matter
- to share your experiences in a meaningful way with all you meet.

What I learned along the way will provide you with a starting point and practical advice that you can use to identify and develop *your* life values and some useful communication principles and conversation habits i.e., those with no judgment or anger - with curiosity and genuine interest. I invite you to recall those conversations that have blocked, upset or caused you anger or distress as well as damaged other people.

Let me ask now that you release those memories and create a new daily 'magical conversation' practice for authentic harmony through a practice that is steeped in happiness, joy, mindfulness, new discoveries, and wonderful relationships.

I call these Magical Conversations. In this book, we will discover together that sharing wisely and without judgment is how you will release your power and attract authentic harmony to shine more brightly on a dark turbulent sea and invite others to your sacred space to co-create a new future.

Imagine you are a lighthouse and although you are grounded, solid in the foundation rocks at your core, the sea is violent, and many are drowning. Rather than jumping into the rough waves without a life jacket and potentially drowning, you can shine more powerfully from the source of your life lessons and invite everyone who passes to sail *authentic harmony* oceans to the calm waters of safety. Hopefully, this light brings with it joy and laughter, and a good sense of your authority about who YOU are – as you sail on with a selfless ego and with everyone's blessing!

Not *all* conversations will be magical; they may melt into arguments, debates, conflicts, fights and even wars.

With practice, however, you can create mindful conversational habits that lay a path toward *The Power of Authentic Harmony*. This power starts within you and is yours to use not to control but to serve, support, and succeed in all you desire aligned with your traveling companions. To train your mind to flow and adapt your best natural self, this book offers appropriate tools and techniques, aha moments, and shared advice from my own life and others.

This book is practical, full of commonsense, and seeks to set a tone for conscious and magical future happiness and authentic harmony if that is what you choose. You will find that the future is less about words and more about experience. Whatever you do now, always remember your choices are yours, the words are yours and your reactions are the seed of your future life.

ACKNOWLEDGMENTS

My gratitude to all who have inspired me to bring Magical Conversations out of the magician's box at this stage of my life and to know *The Power of Authentic Harmony* in my own life journey. Special thanks to my daughter Gemma for officially naming me as one who *"creates Magical Conversations"* back in 2008. I am honored to do so and am always inspired by her natural wisdom about people and communication styles. Thank you to my son Ben and my son-in-law Frazer who have both shared valuable insights with me as to how men of their age perceive conversations that matter. Thank you to my husband Jim for engaging in a special Magical Conversation in 2011 when we met quite serendipitously in Budapest, Hungary. His love for me and his belief in my work has brought me to this time and place. I am thankful for my entire family, and all my wonderful friends and colleagues. They have each influenced my life's journey which has included thousands of conversations and the knowing of my power to inspire authentic harmony in those around me. Each one is an intricate part of my story.

Thank you for those in the UK, in Malaysia and now in the US and across the globe via zoom during these turbulent pandemic years – and with all whom I have had the privilege of connecting, collaborating, and working with on various projects across a range of businesses … friends who shared my vision to welcome new narratives that say *Goodbye Equality-Hello Harmony,* suggesting the lead from a women-centric perspective that welcomes men to a new conversation game of life.

As I have resided, during my travels, on three continents, I have had eye-opening opportunities to observe and communicate with new perspectives on different cultures that are worlds apart. For all these amazing conversational experiences, I am so very grateful. What I learned first-hand; I can now share with you.

TESTIMONIALS

Dr Pauline, the great communicator, has captured into words what many of us have tried and failed. Through this book, my eyes have been opened to an amazing method of communication that breaks through barriers. It was an informative, fun read and as someone that handles and interacts with different personalities daily, being able to apply these methods turns normal conversations into magical ones. **Dr Nor Fariza Ngah, National Head of Ophthalmology, Ministry of Health Malaysia**

Dr Pauline works like a world-class cook in a resort kitchen by creating authentic harmony for the workplace. She blends any number of elements to create a winning recipe! **Martin CJ Mongiello, USA President, Rotary Club of Global Impact, Former White House Chef**

In the unfolding challenges of equality and the drive for open conversations, Dr Pauline shines a new light on how women can lead men to a future of authentic harmony. As a leading champion of equality, I salute her notion that we can resolve any topic if we listen and share without judgment. **Dr Yvonne Thompson, UK Founder WINTRADE Global Women Entrepreneurs Network.**

Dr Pauline has a natural ability to take an idea, thought, creativity, conversations, and dreams into something magical. Magical Conversations transform your being. She writes with unwavering sincerity and complete professionalism. **Dr Veronica Shepherdson, Malaysia, Principal Oaktree Scholars, Entreprenology PhD**

"The lens through which Dr Pauline Crawford views corporate inclusion and diversity challenges is so empowering and achieves bringing different worlds together with love, empathy, and respect. I have learned so much from our conversations and have forged deeper bonds with previously challenging colleagues. **Phumza Dyani, CMSO, Founder PANFID, Women in Leadership Award, Founder She-Unleashed.**

Dr Pauline has a unique ability to understand the very nature of male and female interactions in the workplace - particularly at leadership level, where the dynamic can be challenging. Her extensive work in this arena, where she has created powerful models demonstrating the considerable benefits of more open, empathetic, and inclusive conversations that have real impact on organization culture is needed more than ever in this post covid world. **Peter Thomas, Interim Board & C-Suite Leader. Cross-Sector specialist**

CONTENTS

1

MY NATURAL GIFT TO CONNECT

As children, a great deal of what we do naturally sets us up for what we do innately as adults. Those natural creative talents or gifts, born with you, often seem to disappear as you are influenced at school and are guided by well-meaning, or otherwise, parental controls. Valuing your gifts is the key to why you are who you are today. Do you know your natural gifts?

Ever since I was a young girl, my natural gift has been to connect and chat to anyone who would take the time and listen. Another formative aspect that came naturally for me was to be a bit of a *tomboy*. Today this is not *PC* to say! However, it was how I saw myself. This made me feel different to many of my girlfriends as we grew into puberty and young adulthood.

During my childhood I didn't enjoy dressing up as princesses or having tea parties with my friends and their dolls. I much preferred climbing trees, riding my bike, building dens, and playing football or cricket with my brothers and their friends. I dreamed of being a sailor on the high seas when other little girls dreamed of being a ballerina. Don't get me wrong... this doesn't mean that I didn't enjoy being a girl; I assure you that as I continued to grow attracted to boys, that attraction was reciprocated. I grew into a love of dressmaking and dancing, family gatherings and parties. The main feature in all my relationships has been and still is connecting people and gaining an easy way of using conversations that helped everyone feel good about being together. I also learned that I did not like conflict, and I became good at mediating my way through times when this occurred. I did not always do this well in the beginning as I used an avoidance tactic when I was young.

As I grew to know myself however, I learned the magic of an open mind and principles that I will share with you.

I became determined to improve myself every day and had started my self-reflection by the time I was a teenager. This required a great deal of observation, analysis, and evaluation. As I traveled this path, my natural gift of connection created attraction and I had friends coming to me, asking me questions about this and that, and wanting my advice.

Girlfriends wanted my advice on boys, and the boys came always asking for advice on girls. It was as though I could *magically* tell them what they needed. In hindsight I know now I merely held a safe space for them to share. I didn't realize it at the time, but all those elements were gently nudging me to choose the path where my natural gifts were working, and my experiences (internal as well as external) eventually led me to be a people developer.

In most ways I consider myself to be an ordinary young woman but one possessing an extraordinary desire to serve people. More specifically, I help others grow their confidence and communication skills. Of greater importance, however, is the nature of my involvement. I work with people to help them determine *why they are who they are*. That may sound convoluted, but it really isn't. In fact, this is my own personal journey down this path... *discovering why I was who I was*... that helped me discover my passion to bring what I learned to everybody wanting to find the answer to all their truly big questions in life that start with... WHY?

It's amazing how much a person can learn through the simple and basic act of observation. It was through observation that I was able to see the variations and individual differences that make each of us unique... that make you, for example, stand out even in a crowd. Why? Because each of us has some very distinct characteristics some of which may even mandate, to a degree, certain feelings into behaviors. The way we express those feelings as we begin to gently, or in some cases not too gently, add love to the mix will generate key emotions. Let me reiterate, at this point, that I say this based on my first-hand experience.

As a teenage girl I was more than a little awkward when it came to understanding my fears, emotions, & feelings core to that of a teenager, issues that were constantly invading my *safe space* during this period in my social development. I didn't understand any more than any other girl or boy my age, and I'm pretty sure this was what compelled to me to develop a look and demeanor that told my peers, "Am I bothered?" The message that I inadvertently communicated was, "I know how to cope because I already figured it out." In retrospect, I think this dismissive and cavalier attitude that I was able convey; initiated by my introduction to new people…who seek greater understanding not just of the world but of themselves.

As time passed, I did what most people my age did… I attended school, traveled around England on family holidays, completed my mandatory education and then went off to university. After graduating university with a dual major in Sociology and Statistics, I found a job at a travel company and set off to see the world, among other things. In the ensuing years I married my university boyfriend, eventually gave birth to a son and then a daughter and became a working parent like my husband at the time.

I am proud to be a lively baby boomer and have had many adventures. After I amicably divorced in my late 40s, I threw myself into my own business which focused on people, work, and cultures. My core purpose was, and still is, to encourage men and women to behave with a healthy high-performance mindset, be self-motivated to achieve yet connect with each other in a collaborative heart-values-based collective conversation. I recognize these my evolution of Magical Conversations reflected my natural superpower to 'chatter,' and this has shone a light on my current understanding of *The Power of Authentic Harmony.*

I met my second husband, Jim - an American musician and educator - in Budapest, Hungary late 2011 during a conference that neither of us wanted to attend. I had been single for 16 years after a 30-year happy-go-lucky life with my first student boyfriend/husband and although with a degree of sadness leaving that relationship, my soulmate was out there in the world somewhere. Little did I realize I would meet him in such a serendipitous manner.

We were then 62 and 67 respectively and, had it not been for our love of travel and adventure, our meeting would not have happened. I wonder if it hadn't been for our Magical Conversation that he and I had during the breakfast period on the conference second day, we might never have been married within 12 months at a wedding chapel in Las Vegas, Nevada with an Elvis Presley impersonator singing at the ceremony. Since then, we continued our travels, circumnavigating the globe in the process. In addition to the countries that each of us has experienced in our lifetime before we met, we lived in Malaysia from 2014 through 2017 then we relocated to the United States, taking up residency in Southern California. In March 2019, we came to Las Vegas, to live in the desert under the gaze of the Nevada mountains!

The key lesson I learned from then to now - transitioning from housewife to an entrepreneur; to an educator and an international speaker – is that *people are people* everywhere and many human relationship issues are the same no matter the cultural overlay. My natural gift of *connection* means that I seek to converse so that I can discover more about the other person and build a relationship through that an exploration of commonalities and differences. My natural gift is ever present and as I travel to different lands and meet different audiences, the only challenge, across cultures and all diversity, is a person's intention and willingness to grow and engage with me.

I have developed my own self-esteem and confidence over my lifetime, determined to know my value to me and others. My good and bad experiences continue to drive the changes that I have yet to go through and desire to achieve. Core to all my life and shared in my work delivery is *The Value Creation Cycle*. It's a philosophical - spiritual and practical - cycle that influences my whole life. It functions on the premise that only *I* create *my authentic value (my power)*. The *I* - or you might say, *'me'* - factor is key, and I teach my clients to be open-minded and take a long...and very objective look in the mirror… literally.

As awareness grows… and it will if you are willing… and you begin to smile and value your physicality, your biology, and your cerebral mindset preferences. As you recognize and acknowledge your natural personality, your innate talents (gifts) will bloom. Only then can you further realize your capacity to add value to relationships and to your life. The 'me' influences the 'you and me' (relationships) and gains momentum for the last part of the cycle, the 'we' impact on your community and business life. The value cycle creates the understanding that you are responsible for all things in your life. Over time the magic of life evolves with you in the driver's seat.

My natural gift of connectivity and conversation skills has grown from my natural persuasive skills and desire for harmony. Over my life adventure this has evolved, I have now become known *The Conversation Game Changer.* I embrace this fully and seek to educate and inspire women and men to a new mutually loving humanity game.

It is time for you to assess your natural gifts and realize how these are easy to own because they are yours and no one else can take that away or own them. If you embed these into what you do and, trust me, magic will arise. Your natural gifts well used bring you joy and confidence to remind you who you were born to be. This awareness is not taught at school, in fact often deliberately dismissed and ignored in the traditional education system.

A simple example of my own natural gift is my authentic smile.

At the age of 17, I remember sitting looking into the mirror, rating various aspects of my face, eyes, and hair. I noted in my handwritten diary that as I looked and felt better when I *smiled,* which I loved to do so that would be my gift to my world. Sounds straightforward now, yet it is an element of my presence that is frequently complimented on and adds to the magnetic magic of my presence. It is a gift I have deeply embedded in my persona and is as natural as breathing for me. Everyone can smile, you can too, yet I observe that many do not. They wait for something to smile at!! I even wrote in that diary *"I am surprised adults do not always smile and this is sad"* In my naïve youth I had yet to discover the conflicts ahead that weigh people down and make that smile disappear.

With my clients over the last 3 decades, I have asked them to assess their natural gifts. Through countless seminars and workshops, I find women can be quite dismissive of their natural gifts if they deem them to be less valuable in their workplace experience where learned skills are the major credential.

These natural gifts are essential to the energy we bring to work; being a natural *cheerleader*, a natural *inquisitor*, a natural *connector*, a natural *organizer,* or a natural *caretaker* of other's needs, i.e., a natural '*feelings oriented*' human being. Whatever profession you have, is it from your natural gift set? Women are often born with these '*feelings oriented*' gifts as well as gifts such as natural *cook*, natural *artist*, natural *mechanic,* and so on; the list is endless.

Men are often confident of their natural *physical* and *mental* gifts e.g., mechanic, artist, footballer, dexterous with hands and feet, ability to map and complete tasks etc., yet they do not easily value their emotional gifts within these activities; such creator, visualizer, being an empath and sensitivity to energy. Natural gifts such as being *empathetic*, being a natural *healer*, gifted at *friendship*, known for a *kind* and *generous* nature, being an *observer* and so many more are *unteachable* skills. These are untapped talents on any resume or job application. These natural gifts cannot be taught and yet are the most valuable and often not measured in materialistic or academic terms in a world where you are *qualified* by your paper credentials. You are different from anyone else. Your fingerprint, and you, are unique. Your natural gifts are powerful beyond measure and part of the magic you can bring to your life and especially revealed in your conversations.

Valuing our differences as men and women is another very important factor for conversation ease. This has become my core focus in my vision for authentic harmony as a personal principle for transformation today. The key to tuning into others, being better equipped to build relationships and create new narratives, which are mutually beneficial, is to value different behavior patterns that can seem difficult to others who are not like you - and, if unattended, can dissolve into conflicts and fight. Situations are difficult not people, yet it is easy for you to assume a difficult stance if you don't value what makes us unique yet equal and different. A complexity to the simplicity that happens when we get things right!

I have always been passionate about helping other people connect through communication and conversations that make a positive happy change occur. As this change evolves, the collective and individual consciousness of people shifts. I observe any conflict melting is an opening for collaboration and harmony. My vision for the future is that men and women naturally balance, flow, and harmonize with each other's natural gifts and *create solutions together*. There seem, however, to be many times when men and women just don't see eye to eye, heart to heart, and words and deeds produce confusion and chaos instead of magical outcomes. I use the term *magical* as an energy to allow the *unbelievable to become believable.* Is there a way to make the unreal real and the unknown to be a space to play in?

My intention in sharing my experiences with you is to enable you to create Magical Conversations for yourself that lead you to engage with *The Power of Authentic Harmony* with all you meet. Therein lies your authentic power (without ego). Whatever type of man or woman you are, of any age, culture, ethnicity, or sexual orientation, the choice is that, as a human being, you can find that harmonious magical communication, without judgment, and respond appropriately to all who come into your life. As you choose to be in control of your conversations (not controlled by or controlling others) you will impact every aspect of your life, your family, community, business, and intimate experiences.

My intended legacy is to share the wisdom of those who answered the call to become aware and wise when dealing with the growing demands of today's world. The territory we all live in is shifting fast and we need to be more aware of the obstacles and blocks where gender mix, the rise of professional career women, the generational merger, the dual income working parents, entrepreneurs and business leaders in contest and cultures clashing can drain our ability to smile. We are surrounded by a social media digital existence that puts everything on show.

My vision is to enable women to listen to the wisdom of men and vice versa in a spirit of mindful loving intention; to allow magic to occur, in the unknown space of all possibilities, and together rewrite the narrative for authentic harmony among all populations, communities, countries, diversities, and inequalities that arise today in a world that feels the weight of potential impending pandemic conditions.

As I face these times with you in an even more chaotic world, I sense that you and I need to address the core honesty required to reach the authentic harmony nature of humans and to seek the balance needed between the *positive masculinity* that drives the operation of our world and provides substance and logic, with the *positive femininity* that nurtures and protects, feeds and cares for us all. The latter feels the pain and healing needed in the universal pandemic suffering in our soul journey. The former seeks to resolve the 'problem' with science and material actions. We need both in real synergy. My mission is deepened in these times as we need can create a combined new narrative, a language of awareness among women and men, separately and together, that focus on humanity, prosperity, and peace as well as economic, social stability and growth for our planet.

Can men and women truly and authentically respect each other when perspectives born over life's experiences are very different? Herein lies our challenge as we ride on the wave of uncertainty from now onwards. Our responsibility is to flow forward from the past battles of equality to the future synergy and *The Power of Authentic Harmony.*

The conduit to this destiny is through Magical Conversations – those conversations with no judgment or anger or the desire to control others - are crucial in this transitional time as we move from traditional life in business to a conscious mindful harmony, where people are valued as human beings not merely business and service resources. In my commercial life, my team and I focus on

Business Consciousness as a core to creating a corporate heart culture that honors emotional integrity at work. Corporate Heart International is my legacy consultancy serving *people* as *the life force* for natural success for sustainable results. Working with clients in different countries, I note that similar hardships, tensions, and concerns arise now when people get stuck in the fear of "when will we return to normal (the past)?" Those who hold the healthy view that the *new* normal is a shift towards people, planet, and prosperity rather than productivity, produce, and profit are better placed to grow sustainable enterprises long term.

At the core of today's shifting world economy, I (and many awakened millions like me) have set intentions to engage both the *heart* and the *mind* to bring emotional integrity to business and synergize all the talents from diverse individuals, men, and women alike, maximizing their natural gifts and unique styles. The purpose in all of this is the safety, wellbeing, and growth of their business and their communities.

If you place this emotional intention as equal and as important as the logical procedures to secure operation excellence in today's fragile global and local markets, I know we can create a future worth living with amazing relationships and healthy prosperity.

There is, however, a leap of faith required from the past if we are to achieve this together. I invite you to imagine a *Joint Custody World* where men and women, of all shapes, sizes, colors, and diversities, to share responsibilities, be accountable, truly listening to the needs of each other, willing to co-create together for the good of all, combining best business practices, plenty of imagination and natural talents/intelligence from all players of the game. Only then will we survive AND thrive. My mission is to ensure this occurs naturally rather than to be controlled by systems, authorities and external forces that censor our natural human energy. Sharing our natural gifts, knowing women and men are equal and different, and doing so without judgment, is a central part of this approach to understanding that Magical Conversations can seed a new landscape, a new game, with everyone's wisdom shared. A foundation guideline is that no-one 'tells you what to do or say" – there is no judgment, only shared experiences, in this space of contributions.

The use of Magical Conversations as a transforming formula to grow *The Power of Authentic Harmony* is a primary process. It leads to potent sources of people's energy and content of life shared that permit a distinct benefit to people and their inner authentic power. When people feel safe to share without ridicule or contention, lives transform. As you shine like the lighthouse to give safe passage to participants in your sea of conversation, you give authority to honesty, trust, and integrity. You become a leader who values life in yourself and others. We are all leaders in some way, leading others to feel safe and excited to shift in healthy co-existence with a renewed energy for collaboration. This formula, laid out in this book, provides a safe, harmonious, and inclusive way to host all perspectives around the table of our intended *Joint Custody World.*

To honor natural differences in our core behavior patterns that naturally occur in conversations, I have developed and researched a range of Gender Dynamics Intelligence (GDI)[©] archetypes and preferences that help the Magical Conversation formula. This is about women and men together and separately knowing who they are and then recognizing those around them who are not like them.

The archetypes are always invited to be respectful of human nature being unique, and honor that "We are all equal but different. I am unique, just like everyone else." Real synergy among women and men is vital for progress together.

The Magical Conversations Formula is to set three basic rules –

- o no judgment – contribute through the lens of your experiences.
- o no anger (or ego) – use passion and enthusiasm in the way you engage.
- o no coercion – do not be too quick to act or control conversations during the time allotted, allow flow to occur .

Once we gain full awareness of self and others, using my GDI©️ archetypes, we can calibrate and enjoy wonderful ease in conversations using natural variables in reactive behavior, communication, and choices in every conversation topic.

You are alive in the most powerful era of possibilities and changing landscapes and narratives. I especially invite women to play a greater partnership and leadership role with men to achieve *The Power of Authentic Harmony* while acknowledging, honoring, and respecting individuality and different natural traits as men and women. Having declared that, I invite you all to explore any difficult topics, daily, in a Magical Conversations manner.

It is time to release the past – keeping the best elements – and seeking the present balance for a future where joint custody is given to women and men equitably – all talents utilized and valued - and with authentic harmony as our mantra.

Think of this approach as comparable to developing all the elements of a great orchestral composition in which everyone can play their part. If you attend an amazing symphony with choir playing your favorite melody, how do you feel? It takes time to perfect, yet the result is inspiring. In this metaphor, you are both player, singer, and audience, with multiple elements that can shift your world receptivity of the music created.

In the Magical Conversations orchestra today, do you know *why* you are *who* you are and the *music* you play?

First assess *who* you are in your natural GDI©️ Archetypes style, observed in the words and deeds you use naturally within the full circle of life's conversations. This is not your gender identity, personality or defined by your sexual preferences or any other diversity categorization. We have studied many aspects of archetypal core behavior - male and female, masculine and feminine - and have mapped the baseline traits into a circle of life in which four archetypes play to their best natural reactive behavior patterns. Let us look at the archetypes we use thought the lens of the orchestra conductor.

Traditionally, we are used to a strong leader, a composer or conductor who is a masculine-minded male, who has written the score of our economic systems for two centuries and more – this is our *Ruler* archetype, action-oriented and requiring accuracy and with a linear *positive masculinity* directive for action. With economies and society changing over the decades, we observe so does the music and the players who influence the resulting performance.

Using the full orchestral metaphor, we find sensitivity being valued in the music score and in leadership with *Philosophers*, intuitive feelings-oriented men, who will understand and embrace the *positive femininity* within their maleness and connect their intuition to women's emotions with gentle flowing soothing music. Do they play in the woodwind section, using smooth sounds that mellow the heart? These men are different to *Rulers* who are more logical action-focused males who play with *positive masculinity* rules, direction, and strength. Maybe if not the conductor, they play the drumbeat or the brass section?

Our female heart-centered archetypes all embrace nurturing and relational energy, and we will find many playing harmony in the string section with a range of violins and cellos – or some in the brass section blowing forth loudly and fiercely. Although all women thrive through relationships, naturally nurturing and caring for others, there are however different preferences in reactive behavior patterns as we found in the males. These preferences add to a woman's emotional behavior when bringing cohesion or disruption to their gender dynamics together.

Let us recognize and applaud the real synergy in the combination of female archetypes – we name these *Magician* and *Sovereign* – and value the *positive masculinity* that is found in our *Magician*, who may play the big band wind instruments, while the *positive femininity* flows naturally in our *Sovereign* whose music touches the heart strings, the violins or flute.

For *The Power of Authentic Harmony* to feed a *Joint Custody World* for women to be co-leaders of economies and families at the same time, my vision is the *Magician* and the *Sovereign* raising their vibration in a supportive loving musical partnership and inviting the *Philosopher* and the *Ruler* to join in with a new resonance for the future message we play together.

To achieve authentic harmony, we must aspire to make our performance so delightful, that everyone will want to join in. We will return to our archetypes in later chapters.

Your natural gifts are innate, use them to the fullest.

These are born with you and, if you use them, they will help you shine.

2

21ˢᵀ CENTURY LIVING

You may scoff at the idea of Magical Conversations...

When you read or watch the news today, in the wake of this pandemic, it becomes apparent that the general population of the world is despondent in terms of the possibility of achieving harmonious conversations between men and women at the top of the corporate world, the political government arenas and within gender groups, many women's movements, men's groups, entrepreneurial networks, local communities, and family enclaves in many parts of our social and domestic world. People alike get stuck into the "I'm right, you're wrong" dialogue and end up either fighting or turning their back on resolutions!

Despite this turmoil I hope you also find a growing groundswell of good stories. Sometimes you must go and search for them, however they are there. Tales of collaboration where men and women creating amazing entrepreneurial and philanthropic ventures work together; of communities recognizing the value of women in the workplace as leaders; of men sharing emotional wisdom and seeking a heart-logic values-based life. Too often these stories are shrouded by nasty stories of male rhetoric and vicious "put-downs" of women, sexual harassment cases and frustrated cries from women concerned about the *bad behavior* of men, especially prominent celebrity, or political figures. It's time to stop this cycle of negativity, this struggle for power, life is a game not a battlefield. It is time to live, not kill ourselves with hate and fear.

It is time both men and women distinguish their ripples of magic before we all get sucked into confusion and spin into mayhem and damage beyond human repair.

Is your life engaged in a whirl of chaos and confusion? Or do you sing to the music and dance with life's magic? We can co-create *authentic harmony* if we understand our natural differences as women and men.

If we all step into this new paradigm of a Joint Custody World, women and men alike will need to choose the mantra "everything is possible." At the beginning of the pandemic, the virus took us into lockdown and mask-wearing, and there was a sharp rise in compassion and care for our neighbors even through closed doors. After two years, of vaccination challenges, ill health, and deaths around us, we have restrictions lifted yet still fear of the virus. Many people have become less communicative. There is more need now than ever to use daily Magical Conversations for all situations, families, and workplaces … and put the most difficult topics on the table. In our round table Magical Conversations format, there is no head, all are contributors, and the topic is in the space between the circle not owned by anyone in control. This goes beyond the traditional learning of rote teachings from the front to a method for engaging people in their "thinking for themselves."

You can influence any conversation and agree on criteria that embrace all perspectives even when not agreed with if you set guidelines of non-judgment and gain permission from all to that effect. You can orchestrate better 'authentic harmony music' e.g., in conversations at home where tensions in teenage years can get out of control, difficult interactions with work colleagues on Zoom meetings, and many more. Can we stop arguing about "what ifs," e.g., what if women were in charge would the economy be better?

What is happening to men within this chaos and confusion of the merger of business with emotions?

The emotional upheaval in the workplace inevitably seeps into your family, social and intimate conversations. Do you stop to reflect before you speak? What changes does this result in?

I have many clients – male and female – who have doubted their ability to get past a stuck point. One leader, a strong female boss, was troubled by her uncooperative staff and senior leads. She was seeking authentic harmony to encourage all to engage in what they each did best. The tensions of misunderstandings and frustrations not shared were draining everyone.

Over six months, we resolved the issues by slowly allowing her staff to speak openly and value themselves, their natural gifts, and their part in the whole and to embed the structure of a Magical Conversation development program into daily working habits. They were essential parts to this process. Each person became aware of themselves in authentic ways, combining *Value Creation Cycle* philosophies with knowing their GDI© Archetypes behavior. They came to understand their differences and how to relate to each other. As they shared differences in the context of their roles singularly and together, they found renewed energy, creativity, and authentic harmony. The whole department became collaborative in a safe circle of sharing, where each was valued rather than critiqued.

Awareness, acceptance then action became their mantra and the boss reported that the results in better working together lasted longer than any other development program in which they had invested. This senior team had believed nothing would change yet it did.

In that program, the sessions covered 6 months, embracing nineteen very different men and women in an HR department in the UK, typical of many workplace cultures where communication had got stuck.

Know that you can turn any conflict situation around. You will discover unknown possibilities are available; you will find judgments can be reframed as lessons on perspectives – and anger-management techniques show up naturally as limited beliefs are shown the door. Your world is changing fast and today is no longer like yesterday. Is it time to change the rules on your negative experiences? Can you use your natural gifts, energize your imagination, seek the unknown and create magic wherever situation you find yourself in? Your only question is "Are you willing?"

It is time to look outside the past restrictions which have created confusion and stopped progress. The WHY seems obvious to me - that living with love-filled values and positive intentions rather than fear-based controls, is the better option. It is the 'how?' That is our challenge. This book is to engage YOU in your _personal_ magic.

Magical Conversations Are Not Soft and Fluffy

These are set with loving intentions for all parties to feel valued, every party to have an equal right to contribute and everyone to understand and respect the rules. Ah ha, you say, … _RULES!_ Yes, simple, and all-embracing. They are - no judgment, no anger, and no restrictive coercive behaviors. No outrageous or harmful _controlling_ behaviors allowed. All parties are to be heard. It should be acknowledged that not every view is invited, and not every view is right or wrong. There should be appreciation of everything contributed and all points should be considered. At the table, no conclusions or decisions are made without consensus or at the very least a degree of observation, patience, and imagination.

Can you feel the magic? The magic is in the mix of contributors, the choice of topics, plus the agreed positive willingness, energy, and commitment to mutually respected outcomes. In a magical conversation circle, everyone is willing to be present and harmonious.

Are people ready to shift their perspectives and be truly inclusive? Many factors come to bear but let me first focus on the GDI© Archetypes so you can break through misconceptions and inspire a more positive approach. Then magic may occur faster!

For over 30 years I have addressed many lively groups; businessmen and women, many solo entrepreneurs, many corporate players, and many owners of small successful businesses, and my theme is always generally about "living a loving intentional life". My encouragement is that you live a fulfilled life whether male or female, at home or at work. My vision embraces all of you 'taking responsibility and ownership for your lives.' A mantra given to me by my parents at an early stage in my life.

I am often asked, by female clients, "how can we bring love and energy into their business existence?" as surely the only way to have a healthy lifestyle existence.

By helping you, as a woman, become a harmonious business professional and attract wise advocates in men you live and work with, you serve both yourself and others especially your sisters worldwide. I encourage women also to attract wise female support as mothers, sisters, friends, aunties, daughters - and colleagues, as customers and suppliers. The goal is to attract multi-faceted, emotionally intelligent, caring, talented, visionary collaborators for your future today. Do not keep the naysayers and negative companions. find

Many men, pre pandemic, were aware or approached with this heart-centered balanced emotional style of living that women desire. Now post pandemic, men are more aware and value the women-centric approach – they see *positive masculinity* as the move away from a toxic reputation that men in business and in many communities have gained due to inequalities that women have battled to overcome. I invite my male clients to practice emotional integrity with women, advocate for their parity value in business and life, and for "women to be women" and not have to act like men to succeed. We educate men about *positive femininity in men and women as a force of nature* that compliments *positive masculinity* is now the sensitive flow business requires to harness the hearts of their employees and their customer loyalty today. Women and men in partnership wins economic stability post pandemic. People matter, women matter, life matters.

My clients learn to share in their best archetypal GDI$^©$ manner and learn how to navigate the tensions that have arisen for women in general not having equality over their lives. Now is the time to shift the paradigm more so men know they are an important partner, in every communication, for recognizing men and women have core natural differences when it comes to *conversational behavior and the path to authentic harmony.*

Today more men recognize that emotions are both needed and achievable to balance the logical mind. This will lead us all to a more awakened balance. Leading with the Magical Conversations Formula allows you, as a man, to expand your existence for the better. Having said that, most men are less likely to have lengthy unconnected conversations. Men tend to get engaged in a topic and lend their views and thoughts focused on that seeking an outcome and comradery. Women may converse similarly but more often they hold conversations that cover variable topics, personal agendas and go off at tangents, employing emotions more readily than men.

If you take a wise stance on all matters and draw on your natural gifts, you will more easily develop personal wisdom to make you more magnetic and an attractive power source. Your natural gifts, as I have written earlier, are your strength and your power, and are uniquely presented by you to others as you engage in conversation. Your success depends as you *knowing you* as you listen and connect with others. The connection is a two-way street. You may be a male or female from any generation and culture across the world. You may have a strong *positive masculine* energy or a softer *positive feminine* energy whatever gender identity you choose. Either way your presence impacts others in every situation therefore know your core attributes inform the success you have with others. Remember the mantra with my client's story, *awareness, attraction then action.*

Women can embrace men and bring their light to shine, and men can share their wisdom with women to uplift their aspirations, and each can inform, influence, and emerge new ways to work together.

My advice to female audiences is to build *collaborative consistency*; play your best authentic power, don't wear a mask or imposter syndrome image, draw the female baton with pride and hand it on to other women around the world with loving generosity; use your whole brain, left and right; open your mind to changing the limitations, rules and regulations and do not hide as your magic evolves.   Let yourself own that special place in the moment and seek to collaborate with other women to find your voice too. Know that women are not all the same. Magician and Sovereign patterns exist in all women as well as our loving nurturing relational core. Under pressure, our reactive patterns differ and therein lies the usefulness of the GDI© mapping to help.

Women - *you have fantastic opportunities now to get involved in business, in politics, in social change and in determining your children's future. Yes, it may be a transitional road to authentic harmony with all men, but it is happening as you sleep, eat, and go out to workday by day. Growing numbers of men and women want a more purposeful world, a world where work and life find a more compatible coalition.*

Be your *Magician* with *positive masculinity* in your femaleness and/and *Sovereign* with your *positive femininity* shining in every Magical Conversations.

Men – *you have the opportunity now to own sensitivity and emotional wisdom. I advise men to stay on purpose to value positive masculinity while honoring positive femininity within their manliness. Share your awakened wisdom with other men openly where you acknowledge your sensitivity and creative nature.*

I am uplifted to increasingly meet wise men, of all generations, who think, feel, and act in a space of conscious awareness of others in the community around them. Men tell me they want to be heard in a new light, to use emotions and to share these without being smothered, to be able to enter the conversation to listen within their timeframe and archetypal style, *Philosopher* with his *positive femininity* in his maleness or *Ruler* with his positive masculinity strength; be aware of your differences as men. We need you both to be wise and advocate for women.

My intention is to set your Magical Conversations rippling out and circling into far corners of your world to impact the globe. This is the light shining from your lighthouse. Let us see how far your message magic can reach. The lessons that follow are keys to success. They are real life messages you can shine to attract great relationships, authentic harmony in all groups and a love-filled intimate life as well as tuning yourself as an instrumental in the growth of good business.

Changing times
impact the need for
care and attention,
so becomes the
change you want to
see. Men and women
living, loving, and
working together in
authentic harmony.

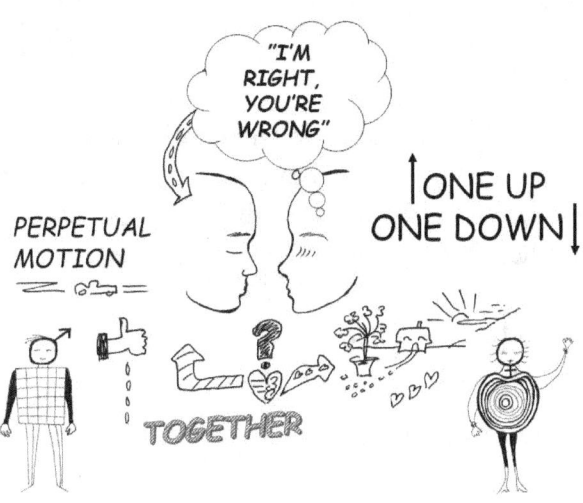

3

LESSON ONE:

Never Make Assumptions

Right or wrong, they will always block your flow!

Are your conversations full of magic or do they pour confusion and discomfort into your life? This is a book of common sense and wisdom drawn from my seven decades of communicating. Ever since I could talk, I have been a chatterbox and looked for harmony in all my friendships. Reprimanded at school for too much chit-chat and challenged by skilled teachers, family, and friends who tell you to listen and learn, now I recognize the true value of a Magical Conversation and the limitations we place on our existence when we speak without setting out to connect and value the other person/people in the room. Too often people in their fear of being 'found out' hide behind control or the 'I'll fix it for you" over confidence.

Without an emotional connection and desire for harmony, speaking to someone can be one-way communication. Intentional 'authentic harmony' conversations are quite different, these turn into magical ones. Whether it's a conversation with a soulmate, a boss, a colleague, a close friend or the checkout attendance at your local supermarket, the conversation experience can be magical and creative or confusing and misleading.

Let's explore what's going on and don't make any assumptions about what will unfold as you read further. It's all about connecting and feeling the connection. When it works, it's magic!!

Have you ever noticed that people who make assumptions and talk loudly on an issue do not encourage a flowing conversation in response? They deliver their communication with an affirmative "I'm right… implying "you're wrong."

They don't invite a response yet may demand attention. This is not magic to me. It can turn into confusion, blocks, arguments and, often, a negative experience.

This happened to me in one breakfast meeting with a potential contact I had been observing as a resource for my business - a business focused on enhancing people's daily performance through conversation excellence. I had the pleasure of being in his workshop the previous day. His style was what I would call "breakthrough with toughness." I enjoyed the substance of the program but not his abrupt attacking style (my perspective). I was there as a willing participant and went with the flow but felt he placed me into personal conflict too readily. As we set at breakfast for the second day's program, he fired questions at me, loaded with assumptions a) that I was there to listen - which I did - and b) to tell me strictly about himself and how I might work with him!

As the firing paused, and he eyed me fiercely, I set off on a slight tangent to set the scene for possibilities of work. He stopped me quickly with a statement I will never forget "Pauline, I don't think YOU realize who I am and how expert I am and … we're not having a conversation, I am talking to you!"

I paused for breath, sipped my tea, and looked him straight in the eye, responding; "Your program is excellent (truthfully) but whether we work together or not will depend on my client's requirements." I stopped talking, sipped my tea, and said no more. No conversation is required and such a good example to me of the different energy forces when you're engaged in communication. It's about connecting and feeling the connection, remember? Our relationship was doomed. He stood up, offered a handshake, duly taken, and said "Good we understand each other." I was quite astonished!

I have no idea what he thought we agreed on or understood. I would never work with him. Whether had I been a man, we might have done a deal, I will never know. For me this reminded me of my need for a more inclusive style that I desired for my life and what I did not want. My perspectives were important and valuable to me. In business terms, this meeting was a failure to connect with no way forward. How often do your one-way dialogue patterns such as this stop the flow of your business?

Although his *Ruler* directive had made various assumptions, and his intention may have been correctly delivered in his mind, it landed in a straight-line projection on me (the designated audience), and it crashed into a huge misunderstanding. The only way to receive an assumption is to agree or disagree, the latter often producing an argument. The former can create a dialogue, which may in turn into a discussion and in the end a lively conversation depending on how you handled the original assumption. If you fight it, then you'll have an argument or debate. If you agree and it's not your view, you will end up controlled. I have long since practiced removing assumptions from my life, however, they do creep back when I am not paying attention to the flow I desire.

In this example, I did end up contracting his colleague with one of my top clients. He was a *Philosopher*, a receptive facilitator who understood people, and we used the excellent content that the *Ruler* had created with him. I want to assure you at this juncture that there are many wonderful wise *Rulers,* my colleagues and clients and family members, who are the best advocates for women and *The Power of Authentic Harmony.* (I have two in my Corporate Heart team currently). All the archetypes can be positive or negative. Yes - all of them. I will reveal that later.

A Magical Conversation is one where the flow is circular, interactive, fluid, creative, engaging and no one person is controlling the airwaves. When everyone is contributing freely and without conditions, then creative outcomes emerge naturally. This is a growth potential style for business and life; a win-win situation.

For every conversation you wish to keep alive, and especially a Magical Conversation, assumptions are a block rather than a good start point.

I learned my conversation skills decades ago, starting long before there was digital activity adding a certain level of instant gratification and text communication. Now we all use smartphones and social media, conversations arrive in varied formats. What really mattered, in my early years, was that most conversations were face-to-face and so immediate interpretation happened at a feelings and facts level.

My best conversations came when there were no assumptions, judgments, anger, or external controls. As a little girl who loved to chatter, I gained my natural guidelines early on but often failed to enjoy the experience if my self-confidence was attacked. The perpetrator was often unaware of the attack. If I couldn't contribute useful knowledge, views, and ideas (even when I had them) I would stay silent and unheard. I didn't realize, until later in life, how magical I could make my life merely by believing everything is possible, having the confidence to know my wisdom, and valuing a sharing style of talking and listening that became inclusive, compassionate, and authentic.

Earlier in my life, I totally wanted to say everything with youthful honesty yet often in my naivety, didn't dare say what I wanted to say in case of ridicule. At that time, it seemed unbelievable that I would eventually bring my natural chatter to be my future gift to the world. Surely magic tricks are like that. Presenting the unbelievable as believable!

How did this change cause me to move beyond my lack of confidence? Well, it is a life journey we all can take, and whether you are an introvert or extrovert, the first step is a willingness to engage in self-discovery and take the necessary steps to achieve success. Learn as you grow as well as taking in knowledge. Your history is part of who you are now. Value the lessons learned.

For me, born in 1949, telephones were attached to the wall, letters going via the post and telegrams being the fastest way to send messages, I was privileged to learn conversational skills in a pure and utterly deliciously loving home environment of 'chatter'. In an era where children were told to "be seen and not heard" I was incredibly lucky to grow up in a conversation-rich, happy, loving family. I am born to converse and connect with people, places, design, and ideas, use my imagination, and grow dreams. I have always seen the world as an inter-connected set of elements; me, my physicality, my emotions, my friends, my family, my colleagues, my designs, my ideas, my service nature. I see things in both logical and sequential flows, life to me is a simultaneous *'and and'* experience of probabilities and possibilities.

Over my lifetime, I have loved connecting the dots. Not surprising to you by now, I was a natural mathematics student, I found happiness in those childhood games where you literally 'joined the dots' 1,2,3,4,5 to a 100 and, as you closed the sequence, the character on the page is revealed. As my maturity evolved, I loved simultaneous equations and started to imagine pictures, designs, and scenes without even putting pen to paper, the numbers, dimensions and shapes rose from the page in front of my eyes. I see shapes connected, design in my head, see maps as pictures, lines and spaces aligned and inter-woven into the fabric of every day. These things woke my creativity in dress making from an early age.

Constructing clothes was, and still is to me, a jigsaw puzzle coming together. Having the end picture before you start is key. This is how I came to realize what I now share with in this guide to, what I call, the art of Magical Conversations and why this path led me to understand The Power of Authentic Harmony and why we need this today more than ever in my history and yours.

As the middle 3rd child of four, I always felt connected in a stream of experiences. I remember so many conversations with my elder brother admiring his handsome lead, my sister forming those close bonds that females create together, laughing and chattering, and childhood games with my younger brother, climbing trees and playing our stories out in the garden tree house in North London. There was always a great deal of authentic harmony.

The most concentrated informative time that I received 'conversational skills' was in my early school learning. This was making connections as I formed friendships in the classroom and playground. I discovered that I had an innate ability to converse and, even though shy, I had an unbounded enthusiasm to be first in attendance every day in my school classroom, so I could meet and greet, listen, and connect with everyone as required. It was a natural role I placed on myself, and it set the intention for my later life when I became a well-known and prolific networker, weaving connections as I created my entrepreneurial career. Now via the internet I can do so even more directly in my global experiences.

At school, I became the source of information, the conduit through which people left messages for others and shared secrets. I became the confidential ear for those stories that needed to share yet I held onto my mission to resist gossiping as is often endemic in girl's schools!

In this time, my early passion to help people help themselves came forth. Being surrounded by a large and happy family, who indulged in many British-style tea parties, annual vacations together, and many picnics and fun outings before fast-food joints and smartphones changed our lives.

My two brothers and sister and I were encouraged to be familiar with those visitors regularly entering my parent's home. Also taught to be welcoming, we helped in serving others in all festivities, and to perform a party piece to the assembled family and friends' audience. As I grew into a gauche teenager, I was expected to join in, listen and converse with adult aunts, uncles, grandparents, cousins, peers, and a wide range of friends of the family. A rich environment to learn about conversations. As a naïve soon-to-be adult, I listened and learned assorted styles; some direct, some indirect, some fierce and angry, some soft and gentle. Many assumptions would be unchallenged, yet others would provide a lively open-minded discourse on a topic and explore the whys and wherefores of everyone's experiences. The latter were my favorites and informed my mind, my curiosity, and my interest to deepen my awareness of those subjects that resonated with me. I was young and naïve yet always keen to learn. I learned early on in life that I did not like assumptions, they always got me into trouble!

When I left home to go to university, I continued to hone my conversational approach. I soon learned that I attracted a wonderful group of friends, mates… boys and girls who were eager to get together and 'chew the fat' as they say in Britain.

My career progressed through the 1970s and 80s through a post-university marketing role in a lively young mixed workplace, and then onto joyful years giving birth and growing my young family, two kids to my university boyfriend now husband. We moved around the UK, from London to Bristol, to the Cotswold and country life with his job. Here I landed in a small village (population of 200) with two young babies and a whole new existence. I set to create my conversation network and soon, like my school classroom, I became the central source for connections across two small villages (circa 1000 total population).

My role as a connector, communicator, and conversationalist was bubbling throughout yet I had not recognized the power of my experience.

After moving back closer to London, in the 90s I became an Image Consultant, and Entrepreneur and founded Corporate Heart in December 1999. Over 30-plus years this is now Corporate Heart International and based in the USA. My passion has always been to educate employers and employees of the nature of healthy high performance, authentic harmony, real synergy among women and men, and - of course – in Magical Conversations!

As I look back now at my endeavors, the nature of conversation and harmony are at the center of building my great relationships, teams, and workforces. The natural application of my own archetypal style to the conversations helped me to create the harmony I desired. Today we live in a relational world. Your relational skills are vital in your leadership toolkit as business shifts and emerges into a different more communications-based agile digital global market. Since 2000, with the rise of our digitally connected world, Facebook, platforms like Google, social media, and global visibility, we converse all the time online. Due to generations and cultural diversity, the growth of women into business and entrepreneurial careers, everything has shifted.

The objective of Magical Conversations is to harness the heart of human connectivity in the words and experiences we share without judgment and in a safe space of sharing. I fear that this art has been lost during our fast-paced profit-oriented world where time is money, and conversations may be seen as a waste of action time by some.

We don't always respect the time and people we are around. Both home and business are reduced into bit-size-texts. Full sentences do not seem to count, and grammar takes a back seat to action while the pleasure syndrome of the 'what's in it for me' is rampant.

Has the art of non-judgmental conversation and the desire for authentic harmony disappeared?

We find ourselves in a world at war...literally and figuratively...with so many arguments and polarization of opinions on so many topics from climate change to racial tension, and a rising voice for women's empowerment and the end to violence, we have much to resolve. I believe we have focused on *What has gone wrong* rather than - having survived the pandemic - *What should we be doing together to make a better more harmonious future for all?*

In 2008 I was working as a consultant to corporate clients in London and was working across the UK. A confessed workaholic, enthusiastic about my work, networking, connecting, conversing, creating attraction, I aimed to encourage my clients to enjoy their natural gifts and perform to their best. My engagement style was friendly, intelligent, and full of smiles. I would often become friends with my clients as a natural part of my teaching healthy high- performance techniques. I would receive compliments on my style of engagement inclusivity. I was happy. You may or may not have guessed by now, I am a *Magician*, with a great dose of *positive masculinity* in my feminine femaleness, I love logic and action, as well as designing concepts and connecting ideas and people. However, I didn't always make the hard sell others suggested I do.

My best contracts came unexpectedly as I conversed with my usual animated enthusiasm. One day my daughter Gemma, said to me after a particularly magical conversation we had had, where whatever I said made good sense and resonated and created an ah-ha moment for her, "Mum, you should call yourself the President of Magical Conversations." the ultimate compliment and I accepted. As I contemplated the title, I decided that 'Ambassador of Magical Conversations' was more apt.

I printed a simple business card with that title and forayed out to the London network scene with confidence.

I remember, soon after that, a lovely summer evening, one of those beautiful, rare times in London, a sunlight rooftop network party. Magical indeed!

As I handed out my new card persona, I became delighted to hear positive responses. Did the need to enjoy such conversations come from a desire for the unbelievable to be believable? Was life so tedious and regular, or even stressful and draining, that the thought of such conversations an offering that irresistible?

That first time; an all-female audience. So once more I trailed out my title to a networking garden party in Soho, full of seriously suited men and women. As a client lawyer approached, I shared my card, and she expressed her delight as she knew me well. Her lawyer husband approached us and as she turned, and announced me to him, my heart sank. "Surely he will be skeptical about this," I said to myself. In receiving the news that I was The Ambassador of Magical Conversations, he immediately responded affirming that "this is exactly what we need in the law arena." I was bowled over, delighted, and excited. What I realized then and since is that people react positively even to the suggestion without knowing what the *magical* part means. They know if their life does not have it; they are sure they need it; they want it and they hope it will be joyful in its outcome.

Having gained positive responses from men and women alike, I can assure you even the mere idea of Magical Conversations intrigues and delights people from all occupations.

The time has come for me to act on my discovery and over the last decade I have run workshops, seminars, and programs on Magical Conversations. I now have a decade of experiences, workshops, and magical conversation circles to share with you. I bring you not just the formula but the principles, values, and experiences I have had to ensure it works for you every day.

Make no
assumptions and tell
no lies. In the
moment, always be
ready to respond to
the unknown, the
impossible and the
magical. That will
make possible all
that you wish for.

4

Lesson Two:

Set Well-Thought-Out Loving Intentions

Do you want a conversation of love or fear?

If you focus on the two core emotions in all conversations, you will notice LOVE (positive) and FEAR (negative) rule your thoughts, words, and deeds. Your core quest in starting, joining, or ending a conversation is the intention you bring and to what goal or objective you have for both the conversation content and flow and the relationships that occur through your actions. In reviewing your conversations, what emotions do you face more often, LOVE or FEAR?

Interestingly, both LOVE and FEAR produce results and will influence decisions. FEAR, however, damages the user/abuser as well as the abused, but the abused user will, in most instances, be the more adversely affected. More than that, a destructive conversation is not magical and can turn into an argument or fight. What is the outcome for you if you allow *loving* to dissolve to merely *liking*? It may be OK for a while however it may decline to *disliking,* falling into *loathing,* and moving towards *hating.* That conversation journey takes you to a fearful place.

The power of choice is within you whenever YOU choose love or fear as your guide. The ensuing emotions compelled by LOVE are positive because they come from being in a loving intention state with another human being. These emotions include joy, passion, compassion, respect, trust, empathy, and authenticity... you can continue to add any positive adjectives you identify with. These augment the possibility of mindful, conscious, loving, living and meaningful conversations that attract magical results. In short, your enhancement is the art of keeping loving intentions alive in you and your conversations, aligned with your values shared with others.

You are "in charge" of your state of mind, body, heart and soul and the choices you make every time you enter a conversation with the intention of magical outcomes. In my experience, understanding life runs on these two emotions love or fear, and all emotions derive from these. Your choice is the key to your happiness and success in most things you want to achieve.

Magical Conversations are infused with loving intentions even when focused on serious matters. You can only grow within the core of your being when you are in a balanced, harmonious, mindful, and loving state. Surely, you want to have loving, Magical Conversations, don't you? All else originates from this core to dissolve and freeze fear out of your life. Is this possible? In my experience and in my considered opinion the answer is **YES!**

Conversations happen all the time, some are mean, deliberately caustic, angry, and even vicious and deliver chaos and confusion – others are joyful, funny, loving, embracing, creative, and achieve magical outcomes. They range from street smart, and common sense to high-brow intellectual reasoned and innovative – yet all to connect and contribute value. The content of a Magical Conversation is the richness of life and delivers results for everyone that are abundant and flexible. Everyone wins in their heart even when taking away different outcomes. You need to start with valuing where your conversation starts -i.e., with you. Who are you in every conversation? "Before I get to know you, I must know me."

This is not an ego pursuit but a self-discovery and knowledge of "who I am" in any conversation.

You didn't arrive in this world with any words. Babies learn to talk over the first two years, some early or some late, yet all the time they hear words and participate in a non-verbal conversation with their parents and family. Especially their mother. Instructions are received and indeed understood in the first months. As a baby you learn how to elicit responses by crying, laughing, holding on, and feeling the touch of another human being. You receive and understand dialogue long before you say your first words. Your value starts to build at birth (and in the nine months in the womb) in your journey as a human being.

BEING "ME" is your start button for your *Value Creation Cycle.* This is the "I am…" factor. Set the intentions to get to understand yourself, truly and honestly…and that's not always easy, it means taking ownership of your natural loving value, your physicality, your emotional gifts, and your conversation nature. You are the magnet for attracting Magical Conversations to you.

Like me, you may have spent much of your early life lacking the courage to own your conversation as a naïve teenager. Distinguish what you perceive and know yourself to be. You may have listened too often to advice from parents, family, friends, and colleagues who see you through their eyes, not yours. Your early experience is key to your awareness and ultimate acceptance of your natural conversation style.

Although I always loved to connect and chat with school friends, if I felt awkward and clumsy, made a mistake, or got reprimanded at school, it was because I was not very clever, hence my self-esteem and confidence suffered and so did my conversation flow. In analyzing my situation as I grew into early adulthood, and in working to overcome my limiting beliefs, I began to realize that being honest with others…and particularly with myself, about what I did not recognize was as powerful a confidence-builder skill as any learned qualification.

Instead of carelessly opening my mouth to talk, I started to listen and learn more about how to interact in ways that engaged and flowed. I became the authentic harmony magnet!

Conversation is a journey and as you travel on the road ahead, it will unfold before you with YOU as driver and passenger. As you grow in confidence, never stop listening but do know the "I am…" without ego. You must understand that, with a good start, the journey should begin to flow towards recognizing and naturally inviting other people to engage in 'your' mutual conversation. The conversation now 'ours' must embrace all involved or else it's a monologue. It's not about the words as much as it is about the feeling, the experience, and the flow of relating. This increases your magnetism.

You might be asking yourself why you need to relate to another person as you build a conversation. It's more than communication, it is about making a connection. Like electricity, you must place the plug into the socket to find live connectivity. *Relating to others* is a natural input and output of making that connection into a truly magical conversation. It is a great way to develop a lasting relationship. Who do you want to build a relationship with? How do you go about initiating a new relationship? Where would you begin? When will you be able to tell that your conversation is moving into building a relationship? Are you ready to risk your heart by building a relationship? So many questions… so much unknown at this point. The only person you can truly know is YOU and this is a life journey. More on *how to do that* as we progress on our journey in the next chapter.

KNOWING *YOU* – once you know your ME (the *"I am…"*) *t*hen you need to get to know others i.e., the other person/people and build the *connection* mindset for a Magical Conversation. Remember keeping a loving intention in your heart is the easiest way to understand another person.

Seek to understand and value every person you wish to know well and aim to learn new things about them in a loving manner. It is important in your efforts to understand other people that you set your loving intention before you start.

The *"I am..."* you are creating *by being authentically aware of yourself is* expands your ability to *know others* from you heart-center rather than head-logic (assumptions occur here more easily). Your conscious awareness influences words shared. How you value *who you are* in conversation starts at home, with knowing your family and close circle of friends. The nature of your loving energy in tuning into others, who are different to you, is vital if you are to build a flow of authentic shared value. The *Value Creation Cycle*: *'I–you– we'* flow is created to flow towards the full value *together;* the *'sharing we'* conversation exists in shared outcomes that can build deep and lasting relationships.

SHARING "WE" is where the full magical conversation flows into the 'we' outcomes. Take time to sense your joy in the fullness of Magical Conversations in the collective, in the group, and even larger audiences. Sounds simple, doesn't it? But I sense you might be saying to yourself, "My experience is different. I set expectations and they fall short of reality once I get to be acquainted with someone."

The key is to know yourself, unbiased and unfettered (difficult, yes?), and set INTENTIONS based on loving thoughts, feelings, words, and deeds (do you practice this daily?), and to REFRAIN from setting tough expectations. Try this, please, and see for yourself.

Set INTENTIONS come from your heart, your desires, and your imagination. This is what I call being a heart-centered human.

EXPECTATIONS come from your head, not your heart, and are often affected by external forces, i.e., what others tell you.

In my journey, *The Value Creation Cycle* has guided me always to take responsibility for circumstances positive or negative. It is based on an ancient Buddhist principle that I discovered when reading *Tsunesaburo Makiguchi's book "Education for Creative Living."*

His educational experience in Japan over a century ago, showed that young children blossomed more readily and were more creative when they valued their own natural gifts and brought those to play in the way they built value for others and so grew value for the communities. Often your natural gifts are downplayed when you enter the classroom and traditional teaching methods replace your value with a curriculum.

This value cycle philosophy has been a major element in my life success and has enabled me to attract great relationships that are alive, sacred, loving, and loyal to this day. This is part of every client session and program that I have delivered for over 30 years.

As I applied this in my life, I decided to take responsibility for my thoughts, feelings, and deeds every day, dealing with positive and negative conditions with loving intentions - so that I am the master of my destiny. Everything started to transform as I held this cycle in my mind's eye and in my heart and acted on it. It is my mantra for everyday living. There are three steps:

1. BEING "ME" Get to know yourself in every aspect of mind, body, heart, and soul, know the "I am..." that you are born to be.

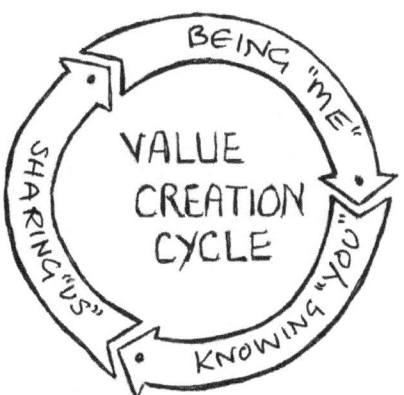

2. KNOWING "YOU" Grow your awareness of others and know why you attract Magical Conversations with another person or group.

3. SHARING "WE" Bond together as you form relationships beyond the boundaries, collaborate, communicate, create our world.

Value the *I am* within you. Be at peace with others. Welcome them with joy, and know their true value looks you in the eye.

5

Lesson Three:

KNOW YOUR INNATE ABILITY TO CONNECT

Connection levels vary with your Relational Quotient and 4Rs

Your words are important, however, your tone and delivery, body language, and commitment to be present in every moment are vital as breathing is to life itself.

Knowing thyself is key; the "I am..." starts the "You are..." which leads to the "We are..." *The Value Creation Cycle* you learned about in the last chapter. Knowing others and understanding differences are the richness of relationships and setting the collective intention is vital for an outcome valued by all. You may be a one-to-one person, a more introverted personality, or a one-to-many stage presence, a more extroverted persona. You may be a mixture of both depending on the situation. Always tune in rather than tune out.

Are you an introvert and avoid conversations? Or an outrageous extravert and overplay your role?

- How do you relate to you?
- How do you relate to others?
- How do you react to people, places, and possibilities?
- How do you risk stepping outside your comfort zone to potential ridicule?
- What overall responsibility do you take for your impact on others?

Let's develop your RELATIONAL QUOTIENT with 4Rs

RELATE-Ability:

Knowing the value of **WHY you are WHO you are.**

How do you RELATE to yourself?

What is your current self-assessment about the positive intentions to honor yourself as the man or woman you are?

Are you a tough, strong, logical male, action man *Ruler* or a gentle sensitive man, theorist, or reflective *Philosopher*; are you bold or shy? Aware and emotionally robust or unsure how to manage these emotions?

Are you the outspoken, logical woman, *Magician*, or the gentle protective woman *Sovereign*; or a mixture of both? Feeling vulnerable or unbreakable? Soft or strong or both?

There are multiple personalities and gender identities of course, however as we focus on our four *GDI*© Archetypes using gender dynamics intelligence to navigate this awareness of self and others: *Ruler, Philosopher, Magician,* and *Sovereign,* our quest becomes easier to observe core behavior patterns on how YOU relate to you and others on an everyday basis.

Are you the type that loves conversations but doesn't listen? Or the one who always listens and then regrets they didn't say anything! Are you someone more focused on *telling* or *asking*? Are you naturally *judgmental* or more of a *perceiver*? Are you a *detail-focused* individual or a *big picture-don't-mind-the-details* person?

Many of you will have experienced filling out profiles that outline your personality and temperament. Type and temperament are extremely important ways to recognize differences and the starting point to learn about YOU.

In addition, if you take a long honest review of your natural gifts, look in the mirror quite literally, take stock of your feelings, accept compliments when they arrive, and know that you are unique - *and so is everyone else.*

In all cases, your ability to speak, your willingness to engage, and your sensitivity to others are primary attributes for creating Magical Conversations and *The Power of Authentic Harmony.* Relax, don't push, and allow the flow to your desired harmonious good life in a positive loving manner.

I accepted that I was a chatterbox, logic-minded, *tomboy,* when I was young and loved talking. As a maturing woman, I knew I was growing into a natural masculine-minded female. My *Magician* nature suited me. Logical and practical in my head, and preferring often to stay there, I was and still am a bold businesswoman who is always confident, especially in work mode, and, at times, a little intimidating!

I learned not to be afraid of what I didn't know and how to admit it if the conversation was making me feel overwhelmed. Now I'm all right with all my characteristics because they are mine. I can ask when I don't comprehend something. I temper my natural style with my intention to have Magical Conversations that flow. I learn new things every time I have a conversation. My journey has been to engage with my heart-center *positive femininity* while honoring my *positive masculinity* and mind logic and my deep passion for harmony.

Today I am stepping up on stage to inspire the world with *The Power of Authentic Harmony.* I am known as the Conversation Game Changer. I do believe we do not need to battle; we need to flow to a future we contribute to harmonize and co-create - women and men together – a new game for a Joint Custody World

I am so much more aware of the factors that everyone can now employ to ensure these are daily occurrences. My experience is here now to help you. If your days are fraught with draining debates, contests on your integrity, reduction of positive affirmations and you are excluded from lively conversations, then start now to relate first to your style and then learn ways to change your conversation habits.

Start with you:

1) Be more aware of your own uniqueness and other people's differences. I balance my conversation strategy instinctively to engage with others as I get to know them. I always retain my authenticity but allow for their style to shine too.

2) Know that everyone has a blend of the strong and the soft, the straight-talking and the soft more abstract approach. Seek to use the words *tell* and *ask* appropriately, especially when different GDI© Archetypes are at play. Men and women are different types and we each respond to words and personalities in an emotional way, positive or negative. Owning your emotional response is key to being in a Magical Conversation.

3) Develop connections at multiple levels, and practice conversations in small ways before you get tangled in larger conversations that may trap you. Chat with the assistant in a shop, build a mini conversation, see if you can make them feel important to you and find a simple connection. Be genuine.

4) Maintained a high degree of self-confidence. I was known as one of the best connectors in business and with family and friends yet in some new situations I would buckle to fear and shut down. Pamper your confidence daily with affirmations, gratitude, and compliments.

I unlearned and unpacked, relearned, and released, and continue to discover more about why and who I am over 7 decades. Many years after my divorce, I remember reaching a state where I was no longer afraid to be on my own without a significant other. I wrote in my journals consistently and intentionally to keep my confidence blossoming. You need to love yourself, in a selfless and not selfish manner, to fully embrace the magic you can attract in conversations and therefore relationships.

At my 60th birthday party in May 2009, I was blessed by the attendance of my family including my 91 years mother, Muriel. In addition, I greeted a room full of amazing friends. I was single, divorced, and happy in my own skin. I looked young for my age; I smiled that day with genuine love and affection for all those who were a part of my world, and I liked *me for me* and for all with which I was blessed. My mother gave a short speech and said I was a "woman of substance" and was enormously proud of me. I was fulfilled on so many levels that day.

Over the years I have systematically peeled back the layers to love my Magician nature and live my truth as a mother, as an entrepreneur, and a world adventurer. I am caring and giving while still being true to my strong, logical business persona. I leverage my natural personal and professional work focused on the science of GDI© Archetypes and my techniques for helping men and women communicate together. I love to work with real-life situations, adjusting concepts appropriately to everyday situational changes. I never stray from my passion, purpose, and vision to spread Magical Conversations wide and far and bring *The Power of Authentic Harmony* alive to build our future *Joint Custody World.*

Here's My Strategy for Relating to BEING "ME"

Awareness Is the First Step

Your approach to **RELATE-Ability** is the start-up fuel for your journey to become more aware of your conversational role in life. BEING "ME" is best when consistent in all your relationships and your conversations. My guiding mantras for "I am… ME":

- **Me**– love and honor yourself, know your passion and purpose and use this to attract others.
- **Me and you**– love and respect partner love and honor friendships.
- **Me and my family**- love and nurture love for parents and siblings.
- **Me and my community**- love your friends and socialize with love.
- **Me and my world**– love and empathize with a mindful love for the communities around you and the world…

Three RELATE-Ability Practices:

1. An Attitude of Gratitude Diary

Get yourself a lovely notebook and a decent pen that you keep precious. Every day, every evening, hand write your gratitude. I am thankful for everything both big and little. Dr John Demartini was the first stage presenter I heard talk about this in the 1990s. He has written his gratitude every day since a young man and built his success on that activity. The power of handwriting your gratitude, the commitment to making a contract with yourself is key. It can be.

A Book of Intentions

Another notebook, this time for your intentions. You can combine the two... no hard and fast rules... yet it's powerful to have a separate book, as this is for stretching your imagination and your desires for life such as dreams, for far-away places, wealth, wisdom, or good health ... and of course for your loving intention to have Magical Conversations every day!

Write down your dreams and ideal goals for your life. Weave a magical tapestry of what you see, hear, feel, sense and desire in your conversational future. You can continue this practice always and encourage others to do so and share ideas and dreams.

Nothing happens by accident although you may need a lot of practice to get to know yourselves and remember you always have free will. Set intentions and watch life reveal naturally!

A Healthy Mirror Image

Take a good review of your current image:

- Get a scrap book, or a colored envelope file, and pull-out cuttings from magazines to collate, select colors and images that appeal and inspire.
- Collect clippings and notes about your lifestyle choices, colors, and shapes you like, the places and pictures you would like to own (or already own), the dwellings and settings where you want to connect with other people and Magical Conversations to grow.

- Take a good look in your mirror, take ownership of your body shape, your age, your health, your weight, your fitness level, and your style. Get to like your natural birthright.
- Change what you want to change (not with plastic surgery though), get the advice of a sensitive image consultant and/or life coach.
- Make some colorful changes to your attitudes and your wardrobe, adding zest to your personal style. Your accessories may be the best starting point.
- Loose or gain a few pounds to find your optimum happy-with-myself weight.
- Remind yourself that in loving me (in other words… learning to love yourself) you are not looking to become egotistical, but humbly honest and profoundly grateful. True, loving, self-confidence is genuine, authentic, and just the way you are, and becomes easy to share sensitively in your Magical Conversations.
- You need to look in that mirror and be perfectly OKAY with who you are. and why you are that way.
- Write down a list of selfless "I am…." statements about you and your natural gifts.

My advice is to be completely honest and realistic and give yourself permission to laugh and cry whenever you wish. I have done this so many times in my life. My mantra is "If something feels wrong, it probably is." I can take ownership and make choices. Feeling good about *WHY you WHO you are* is essential in your journey to a fulfilled harmonious life with others. You are not alone even when on your own.

RELATE-ability goes hand in hand with **REACT-ability**… the next element in our quest to know yourself.

REACT-Ability: Your Reactive Communication Preferences

How you react to others is a critical factor when you meet people and enter conversations. Many highly emotive conscious and unconscious elements occur when you meet others and as you get to know others and share from your heart.

Be honest and look at how you react naturally, it is born with you and an important guide to why some relationships are easier than others. You have learned many reactive modes through your early nurturing years from 0-7 beginning at home with family, parents, and friends, then at school with teachers and peers. Your communication style will be a combination of what you're born with and what nurturing has taught you to use. As an adult, you can become proactive and use conscious thinking and speaking manner. "Think before speaking" is a phrase my father taught me as a child.

Do you tend to react with your left brain (more facts and form) or your right brain (more feelings and future-focused)? Have a ponder on what your first reactions are to these statements, I was privileged to work with Dr Asma Abdullah in Kuala Lumpur. She shared her extensive research techniques with me on communication styles. Here I share a few simple top-level ideas drawn from her work to help you. As you read below, you are drawn to one. You may have two or more - or a balance of all four of these.

What is your primary preference when facing any situation or conversation, are you:

- **Facts focused** … you always start with facts and tend to focus on information transacted rather than feelings.
- **Figures and Form focused** … you need a process or a formula for every process and enjoy things being orderly and in the right place.
- **Feelings focused** … you enjoy using emotion-filled responses and heart-tugging words, and sense emotional states in others.
- **Future focused** … you look to future possibilities, have dreams and desires, use your imagination, and sometimes seem ungrounded.

Reflect on how you react right now to all the people in your life. Notice how others who are different to you are communicating. Observe your own style and how others have different styles to you as you mix and match styles together.

A few clues to follow:

- In a conversation, your **REACT-Ability** may be a clue to unresolved differences that could undermine your conversation. Understand and review your reactive communication patterns, especially under stress or tension. This time spent in observation will be key to your success.
- Do not make assumptions about others' **REACT-Ability** style until you have an open conversation about their preferred ways of reacting. Do share your preference with others through sharing experiences and how you approached each other. If you are a Facts person talking to a Feelings person, you may not get buy-in if you stick to the facts only. Use feelings and words to attract and connect.
- Do not place unspoken expectations on another person before you know them or even when you do! Unmet expectations are often the core issue for many conversation breakdowns.
- Ask yourself: Do you honestly think you can change someone else? You cannot. Are you entering conversations with expectations set in stone? Please do not, you will fail. Bring ideas, intentions, and an open mindset.
- My suggestion (and practice) is to refrain from making any assumptions, judgments, or expectations.
- SET INTENTIONS ONLY and share these with others right from the first meeting. "I intend to get to know you."

INTENTIONS are never wrong (unless the intention is to attempt to change others and that is indeed an expectation!). If you are doing this right, you will find your choices, words and deeds come from your heart. What does your heart desire? What do you value? What will your shared passions be inside the conversation?

It is often expectations that others have of you that harm you during your lifetime. Most of us have had these experiences, whether at school, at a university, in our first job, or from family and friends, when others say; "Do this!" "Don't do that!" These are the result of another's perspective of you ... not necessarily yours.

When you are ready, the conversation will always have the potential to be magical from the outset. The connective tissue between you and others exists. Your success will be the degree to which you are willing to meet others in the mix.

The personal keys to stepping into Magical Conversations in the best way are:

- Authenticity and genuine inclusion in conversations. Do not wear a mask.
- Alignment of words and deeds. Believe in sharing to learn and evolve.
- Transparency and confidence in self-disclosure. Feel safe sharing your experiences and exploring new ways.

Use Your Words and Actions in Alignment with Your Style

If you present yourself authentically and genuinely, with words and actions that are aligned, you will easily open the door to Magical Conversations.

If you have worked on your own defined **RELATE-Ability** and **REACT-Ability** and are sure about YOU, all else will follow.

MY MAGICAL CONVERSATION OF LOVE

When I met my husband, Jim, in 2011, there was an instinctive attraction, a good "relate-ability" factor. Our magical conversation sealed our destiny.

At that first meeting, I was not keen to be swept off my feet romantically. As a practical woman, with a soft heart, and confident persona, I wanted to attract someone who valued me for my intelligence as well as my looks and personality. He valued me, I valued him, two different personalities around the table of love. He has more feelings first, form second, I am more feelings first and facts second and we both have some future thinking for good measure!

RISK-Ability: Your Leverage with Magical Conversations

RISK-ability is an important factor to expand your magical conversation style to engage people especially if as well as being a magnet to attract others, you're genuinely seeking to monetize your conversation's results.

Be the one who sets the different tone, creates the irresistible space that others are attracted to, and embraces fully the loving relationships you gather. This will start to magnetize your message (you) and lead you to successfully monetizing a win in a business conversation or set the scene for a deal to be made and sealed.

Successful business is always built on good relationships and connecting on a personal level. You might have a fabulous and meaningful product or service to sell of course, but your big successes will be drawn from clients who see your magical ability to make them feel magical too.

RISK-ability is always a factor in relationships, yet once you experience the look, feel, sound, and behavior present in a truly magical conversation, you will not want to lose this state. Don't push, allow the pull – the magnet – to work for you. Remember, the following can either undermine or enhance your journey as you navigate your way through conversations and the ensuing relationships you build:

> **Change** – is inevitable and *healthy* if you see it that way,
> **Uncertainty** – is the root of opportunity because everything is up for grabs,
> **Victimization** – is a learning moment if you turn YOU around and stay positive,
> **Adventure** – is the spice of life … both scary and thrilling at the same time, and
> **The Unknown** – invites the essence of discovery, without fear, if you focus on loving intentions and positive outcomes!

RESPONSIBILITY: *Your Capstone to Owning your Success through* Magical Conversations

RESPONSIBILITY is the most important underpinning factor especially when you are setting out to expand your Magical Conversations to embrace a relationship, community, or business opportunity.

Every day chaos and confusion turn up, choices need to be made. Is it easy to give up the magic or will you stay on course when something knocks you down?

How do you deal with the changes in your life to date? Life pressures have changed enormously, for men and women now facing work and home life emotional stresses combined.

Personally, my experience is that many men dislike emotional change, more than most women do but don't talk about it. For both genders, the necessities of life and work - raising families, diverse conditions, and multi-cultural influences on all relationships - have both advanced and drained our potential to maintain a firm grasp on daily Magical Conversations.

For men, engaging with emotional ease is sometimes a strange territory. As a woman, more drawn to overt emotional outlets, females can support men on their emotional challenge by sharing on the same 'together' agenda. Women can acknowledge men's need for solutions as the conversation progresses. Men can allow for fluid flows and often non-sequential lines of thought from women!

Taking **RESPONSIBILITY**, in this context, is not restricted to its commonly understood definition i.e., the state or fact of being accountable. In this book, I invite you to be responsible for your personality and the natural assets you were born with.

This will help you share more as you lead your conversations from your heart center not always your head logic:

- Know what you excel at, and what you enjoy doing, what makes you smile, and what are you naturally enthusiastic about doing. And then... as the world-famous Nike ad says so eloquently... JUST DO IT!

- List those things you do naturally and with ease. Do you write, sing, dance, cook, draw, listen, talk, persuade, design, operate, make, mend, connect, question and research? Are you action-oriented, quiet, loud, detailed, big picture focused? I am not referring necessarily to learned skills but more to those things you do naturally as men and women ...and own it.

- Do what you love, it will ignite passion and help you find purpose so be clearer about your vision for life and be able to share these in magical ways. These are your natural gifts – you were born with these not taught them, remember?

- Do not try changing others to adopt your talents and natural skills. Do, however, inquire as to theirs. Love them for their natural talents because therein lies their treasure trove.

- Make it your goal to find the common ground that you share and the different talents you can add to your conversation, so it flows wider and deeper.

Taking **RESPONSIBILITY** is not always a comfortable task when emotions are getting tense, or relationships are breaking down. You can use a magical conversation approach as a wise invitation to others to release their resistance or fear. Your responsibility is always to seek inclusion and create and maintain connections without controlling, undermining, or suffocating others.

This is the capstone of your Relational Quotient– to take **RESPONSIBILITY** and use your sensitivity and knowledge with loving intentions to connect at a heart level. This was a core principle that my father taught me as a young woman, and it has served me well. At times when I was not sure what to do, I looked at my response-ability principle and signed up to serve the cause or association or business requirement with a commitment from my heart!

Keep these 5 value statements alive by taking **RESPONSIBILITY** for the ...

1) **Open mindset**– I always respond positively to situations as they arise
2) **Choice**– I choose my intentions daily and write/verbalize them every day
3) **Ownership**– I know who I am and open to sharing and aligning values.
4) **Respect**– I am kind and genuine with all people even those who behave badly.
5) **Empathy**– I listen to understand other people and embrace their views.

Make your commitments in the exercise that follows here. Please take this little exercise seriously. I will also ask that you be as specific as you can be. If you do, you will be amazed at the result.

Many hundreds of clients who have taken this 4Rs test and found themselves with an under 3 have been amazed at how a simple test broken down into these components can shift them back onto the path of positive thinking. One client claiming a score of 40 was surprised when I said they got higher scores! The limits we place on ourselves are far greater than external controls. Take time out now to reflect on what you can do next to increase your scores.

I recently received an email from one of my coaching clients from 4 years ago saying she has found my **4Rs** the most pivotal exercise along with the *Value Creation Cycle* philosophy, previously explained in Chapter Four, and yet being in a difficult time in her life, had not acted on the actions and had only now gained a sense of what to do. She said it had changed her life then even though she had waited so long for the light to shine. When the time is right, you will know what to do.

Your Relational Quotient is a combination of all 4Rs – RELATE-ability, REACT-ability, RISK-ability, and RESPONSIBILITY

Try this exercise - Take a piece of paper, and on a scale of 1 through 10, where ***0 = NEVER and 10 = ALWAYS,*** rate yourself on each of the 4Rs. Ask your closest friends to score you as well:

❖ *RELATE-Ability*

0 - I don't RELATE easily to others... 10- I RELATE easily to others

❖ *REACT-Ability*

0- I don't REACT well to everyone... 10- I REACT with sensitivity to another's style

❖ *RISK-Ability*

0- I won't RISK being open and honest... 10- I always RISK being authentic and honest in conversation

❖ *RESPONSIBILITY*

0- I don't take RESPONSIBILITY as it is too challenging... 10- I take RESPONSIBILITY for all my words and actions

Total your score to find your ***Relational Quotient.*** If your score is less than 25 points, I invite you to both ***say and do*** the following:

1) "I *will* improve upon my low scores." List what you are going to do to make this happen.
2) "I am willing to let go of negative feelings and biases." Identify what you will do to reduce and eliminate these.
3) "I am willing to practice the creation of positive thoughts and actions." List ways in which you will achieve this goal.

By the simple act of writing them down, one is far more likely to follow through regarding making the desired changes in behavior.

React from a well-informed viewpoint regarding who you are. Accept a risk, knowing responsibility lies within you. Go with the flow. Do not debate ... relate!

6

Lesson Four:

Authentic Harmony in Every Conversation

Heart-Center Values-Principles for Magical Conversations

From transactional to transformational, from functional, mechanical, and operational through to emotional, intuitive, artistic, and visionary, conversations vary. Recognize the innate factors that influence each person's unique style and the conversational gambits that evoke a mindful, joyful expression of good feelings and pleasure through to the ignition of imagination and mutual excitement.

In the last Chapter, you learned about your *Relational Quotient 4Rs*

Be okay with yourself. Know WHY you are who you are. More than that, be honest with your emotions and appreciate the perceptions and perspectives of others.

Ask those who know you well to share their perception of you. This is a powerful exercise and one not to be taken lightly.

---

1. Ask for *three descriptive words* about your natural style of communication and conversation.
2. Do not ask people who obviously dislike you.
3. Take the positive words and write them randomly on a piece of paper and see where similar words connect. Add yours.

Observe the patterns emerging. Offer to do the same in a group situation, it is a powerful sharing and promotes good feelings. Let people discuss other's perceptions of you too. The more you add positive descriptors, the more you will live into these perceptions. State your words about yourself, allow others to compliment you, and receive these graciously.

My team clients love this process as giving positive feedback to others is often a lot easier than to yourself. It swiftly builds good collaboration and of course, Magical Conversations, all of which will add to business performance and results. A win-win for all concerned.

Seek Magical Conversation to increase your *Power of Authentic Harmony* rather than mere communication.

- Recognize when to adjust your words, deeds, and realities to the extent that others will be able to see that you are working to understand them.
- Willingness will encourage wisdom to emerge as you build a loving intention into your words.
- Practice your *4Rs* and continuously work to keep your *Relational Quotient* at its highest level.
- Knowing *Why you are who you are and how you are perceived by others* are the *two* important keys to sharing with others.
- Ask others, especially those who love you, how they perceive you, invite them to give you three descriptors, thank them without question and note the responses.
- Enter your Magical Conversations with intent to connect and build meaningful relationships, whether for business or social life, family harmony or intimate love

NOTE: Self Love is not in a damaging egotistical pursuit but is developed in a Value Creation manner where you effectively own your positive loving nature. Your success is not about how others say you should be, it's about WHY you are who you are.

Nine Values-Principles to Guide Your Daily Wisdom

In my journey, I have invited many individuals, groups, and classes to share their most meaningful, relational, harmonious, *Values-Principles* that underscore and are reinforced by the natural creation of Magical Conversations. Let me share these collected pearls of wisdom with you. You should know that I have factored these words of wisdom into my daily practices to enhance my *Value Creation Cycle (*Chapter Four). These key behaviors that I know can be owned and used to empower individuals, male and female alike, wanting to build meaningful relationships.

I invite you to add your own, of course. I have found these principles work for me, but feel free to alter or edit them to fit your unique persona, or - as I just said - you can compose your own. Conversation is part of your life and each one of us has a unique perspective that contributes to the journey we're on and to those we meet along the way. It starts with YOU! Remember that if you remember nothing else.

These Values-Principles are an integral part of my intention to lead a loving intentional life regardless of the nature (positive or negative) of those I touch along the way. Whatever you do, make your intentions positive, honest, and believable, making certain that they align with your values... those that *YOU* live by. These emphasize the characteristics and behaviors recognized as unteachable life attributes... ways of being, own them, live them... so that they resonate with you. They have a direct impact on your becoming and being a loving person, true to yourself, and consistent in your world view of love.

Through understanding, adopting, and applying these principles, men and women will be better able to come together to share Magical Conversations.

Nine Values-Principles of Magical Conversations

1. **Authenticity** – Always be honest with yourself. Once you have mastered that, it is of equal importance to *always be yourself.*

2. **Empathy** – This aptitude calls for the highest level of emotional intelligence you possess. You are asked to be able to share someone else's feelings or experiences by imagining how it would feel if YOU were in that person's situation.

3. **Trust & Respect** – Without respect, trust will not come easily if at all. Your goal is to give trust first and receive respect because of earning that trust.

4. **Perception** – This is a belief or opinion - perhaps even shared by several people - that is based on how things seem to be. It is not necessarily factual.

5. **Perspective** – Everybody has a particular way of looking at or considering something and everybody has that right.

6. **Balance** – Achieving a state where all aspects of your life have equal weight and force. When the scale is tilted, something needs to be adjusted.

7. **Transparency** – The quality of doing things in a vulnerable way without secrets. Always be lovingly honest and open rather than guarded and mysterious.

8. **Clarity** – The quality of being clear and easy to understand. Be sure to understand both what is said and - of equal importance – that which may be communicated in non-verbal ways.

9. **Compatibility** – The art of being able to exist, live together, or work successfully with someone else. Using loving intentions as the embodiment of this lost art... will create lasting relationships where none existed before.

With these *Nine Values-Principles* in mind, let's explore how we might build a natural narrative resource, holding our beliefs as roots for positive foundations, heart-centered values on our journey of sharing. The formula of Magical Conversations aims to maximize your probability of success and the goal is to flourish and thrive (not just survive) through your communicating via a deeper understanding of you and others. There are four further aspects to consider.

Passion, Communication Choices, Assets, and Vulnerabilities

It's time for you to communicate and radiate your passion, communicate with impact, assess your assets, and be aware of your vulnerabilities.

Your key to success is to keep learning about your style of thinking, feeling, behaving, sensing, acting, and reacting as you meet, relate to maintain, and nurture your relationships.

Take Stock of Your Current Situation

PASSION

- What makes you buzz with excitement?
- What are you doing or thinking of when you are smiling and happy?
- Are you indoors, outdoors, in nature, in the city, by the sea, with people, one-on-one, surrounded by people, places, and possibilities that make you feel good?
- What drives your purpose and vision?

Don't present a story-book version of yourself and do not try to be someone else. Be honest, be authentic, and be natural. Share your passion, your motivations, and your purpose with those you are interested in.

CAUTION: offer such information in bite-size portions to avoid the proverbial information dump. Express yourself with sincerity… from your heart-centered and intuitive guide. Smile, laugh, enjoy, and be at ease with who you are, keeping in mind how the other's passion and happiness occur.

COMMUNICATION CHOICES

- Are you introverted or extroverted?
- Do you converse easily, or are you shy? Are you able to be open and honest?
- How do you communicate instinctively?
  In addition to what you say, are you aware that you communicate non-verbally too?

Develop the channels and environments that best suit your style, the spoken or written word, music, flowers, outings, quiet environments, or noisy venues. Pick your favorites and share them with your guests. Learn when to stop and listen, and when you listen, invest your full attention. Be authentic, kind, and loving, observing boundaries, especially in the early days of a conversation. Work on developing a no-boundary, unconditional conversation style by opening yourself up so that you implicitly and explicitly invite others to let go of their boundaries too. No boundaries, by default, imply no judgments, no assumptions, and no resistance opening the possibilities ahead, whether business or personal, to be authentic.

Practice being relaxed in your skin and take a class that helps you tune into your body, such as Yoga, Zumba, Thai Chi, Qigong, or Pilates. Feel comfortable with your arms and legs, sitting or standing, and be welcoming with your body language.

With my clients in workshop mode, everyone practices and explores these activities together - from formal handshakes to tabletop meetings, standing on stage or chatting over a coffee, be focused on open body language, good eye contact, and using your hands to support your message (not waving controls) as you host with your own personalized Magical Conversations style

ASSETS

- What do you do best?
- What are your natural talents? *"I don't have any,"* is NOT an *acceptable answer, we spoke of natural gifts at the start.*
- What have you enjoyed doing? What are some of your achievements?
- What are your values? How do these influence you as you journey ahead?

Don't be shy. Be proud of your accomplishments and list them out and I'm not talking about your bank balance! Don't brag about wealth even when making a deal. YOU are your greatest asset. The personal you. Be honest with your personal balance sheet. Be interesting as well as interested in others natural assets. Please, this is not an ego trip, you're not guilty for being talented. Assess your natural attributes. Do you draw, sing, dance, cook, garden, write, compose, etc.?

VULNERABILITIES

- What happens to you under stress?
- How do you cope with rejection?
- What blind-spots are you aware of?
- Who do you turn to for support?

Don't hide away. Permit yourself to be vulnerable, but please do not be a victim. Learn from your potential dark side and look for the light. Failure can be a powerful learning tool in business, in life, and loving relationships. Through rejection or a personal disaster such as departure, illness, or death, our positive practices, knowing and articulating your value principles, and understanding who you are as a man or woman, can help you overcome anything. Your death is the only final exit from the self-discovery journey. Match your actions with your intentions as you choose to overcome vulnerabilities. Hold on to an abundance mindset. There are always more choices for staying positive even through negative situations.

Your **RELATE-ability** is maximized when you are in alignment and fully aware of your PASSION… which set off your value creation cycle adding fuel to your PURPOSE and VISION.

Your **REACT-ability** is the energy that harnesses your maximum communication impact. Remember, your goal is to develop conversations not just dialogue. Conversation only works when it is two-way, three-way, or multi-way!!! You are then truly engaged with each other and your wider community.

Your **RESPONSIBILITY** is to acknowledge yourself by becoming a practiced, principle-led person. Actively work to put the principles into daily practice to transform them into daily habits. Your *Nine Values-Principles* will support and shape your progression and enable you to connect, flourish, and thrive as a loving person.

It is imperative to recognize and honor these elements as a daily practice of loving intentions for yourself and others. There is always a potential **RISK-ability** aspect regarding engaging with others. Why? Because you will always have to face the uncertainties created by other people's VULNERABILITIES too. You have the inherent power to cope with change, facing a wide range of obstacles and challenges from ill-health, financial issues, family tensions, divided loyalties, rejections, and accidents, up to and including the death of a loved one. It is not unusual for such events to occur, and there is no doubt that they can be difficult to conquer.

Be prepared to meet difficulties head-on for your own sake. Value your *passion*, understand your best *communication skills*, value your natural and embedded *assets*, and bless your *vulnerabilities* as lessons to learn from as you journey onward.

I led a special invite to form a Magical Conversation Circle in 2010 with 12 highly accomplished senior corporate players, six males and six females, plus a facilitator to support the flow, a sensitive intuitive male. The evening was hosted in the boardroom of my top client in central London at the time. The topic on the table was "How does gender balance work in the business today." I had carefully invited a range of males and females to share on this.

One of the females, a major PLC bank C-suite executive, was going through a personal crisis at the time with her own board and, unknown to me at the time of the invitation, was feeling marginalized herself because of her gender. Her vulnerability showed up at one point as the conversation flowed onto the imbalance for women in senior roles charged with old-fashioned controls.

The safe space of the conversation circle enabled her to express her emotional concerns and feel good about the vulnerable situation she found herself in. Her gratitude to the circle was shared and applauded by all. A great lesson was learned about being able to be honest with emotions in a business context. If her board had used the same process, they would not have lost a talented senior player. She soon left the post and was headhunted into an even more prestigious board in an international company, one of the most famous in the world.

One guest said:

"Pauline is inspirational! I had the rare privilege of being involved in one of her Magical Conversations in London, together with a group of distinguished business leaders. Her emotional maturity and calm but persuasive leadership style is quite something to behold. But what makes Pauline unique is her deep understanding of feminine energy and intuition present in most organizations, but often suppressed by more domineering masculine energy.

In a world where we seem to have gotten so many things wrong, Pauline's approach to business is a welcome and refreshing lifeline."

Mike Haupt, CEO, Noetic Business

Be passionate, choose well, make wise choices, favor positive results, and value the principles that open the gateway to your authentic harmony.

7

Lesson 5:

A FORMULA FOR MAGICAL CONVERSATIONS

The *Rules* to reach a Joint Custody World

Having worked with many client groups and leaders in companies across the globe, people are fragile human beings who cannot be forced to create or be a good contributor to Magical Conversations if they do not want to. To lead others to a successful life and a business with *The Power of Authentic Harmony* starts with the inner desire to understand others.

My legacy mission is to create a *Joint Custody World*, where women and men are willing to be present *without ego getting in the way*. Now, you may be thinking, surely everyone has an ego, especially in today's cut-and-thrust material world. Yes, we do, it's our survival motor, yet we have a choice to be negative or positive and proactive with everyday events.

Your day depends on whether you are determined to be a healthy mindset, a self-confident loving self (ego), and a decent human being. I have written earlier of the necessity to know, honor, and love yourself unselfishly. This state is key for the following magic and harmony to occur. Having a strong dislike of conflict, I had over my life had to deal with such and developed my rules through good times and not-so-good times.

The *rules* – or you might call them 'guidelines - that I have evolved in my own life - bring about the inclusive style I desired, contain no judgment, no anger, and no-one forcing controls on actions. These became my *rules* so I would be accountable to myself. I have mentioned these earlier in this book, however, let us get clear of the context in which these apply. I call them *rules* because these are not up for discussion if you wish magical conversations to succeed. Once anger hits the table, then the conversation changes. One may feel angry/strongly opinionated about a topic and there are many in the world to be angry about. Poverty, natural disasters, wars, killings, marginalization of women, male suicides, the list is long.

The Magical Conversation disappears *as if by magic* when anger is expressed against another in the circle of safe contribution. This destroys the possibilities ahead. It can be a temporary anger and managed by the circle. To become a Magical Conversation Certified Host, a deeper level of facilitation is taught for serious topic conversations and aligned with a range of *difficult conversation* techniques. The goal is to focus on creative outcomes and mutual benefits where the circle bonds and finds deep trust.

The facilitation of non-conflict resolution methods can be employed and the absorption and melting of anger or any other negative emotion can be managed. The use of Magical Conversations is primarily to invite people to a safe, creative space to share contributions and allow the unknown and innovative to flow to *The Power of Authentic Harmony*. If anger rises, the conversation might continue as a fight, argument, discourse, lecture… whatever it is, it is not a Magical Conversation and so loses the positive benefits.

To ensure that the magic continues, the *rules* are observed, shared, honored, and adhered to. The proactive nature of Magical Conversations means the host or initiator (you) encourages all participating to develop values of mutuality and interdependence. Your priority is to listen and permit others to speak, second is to tune into the environment, the situational issues, and group personalities. Remember there are no difficult people, there are difficult situations of differences misunderstood, and opinions at odds.

As you practice in small ways as you attend meetings, value people during your day with this intention to listen and share and connect. Magical Conversations will pop up everywhere in your day. As you meet and chat, remember you are all partners in the success of each conversation.

Check out your *conversational space* before you start i.e., could be *in the boardroom, the bedroom, the kitchen, or the coffee shop, online or face-to-face.*

The goal, therefore, of the *rules* is for Magical Conversations to be open-minded, joyful, and flowing fully – the experience of the heart more than the mind. Make them part of your life, as I have, and welcome the benefits daily. You will attract amazing friends, clients, and communities. I am blessed to have done so, especially over the last decade of practicing every day the principles and ideas I share here.

This is about real-life, real-world issues, your life, your conversations, your desires, and your dreams. It's not a conversation style learned in a classroom or in an academic textbook. The unteachable skills evolve through experience and your commitment to the life you want not what someone else demands. The key to your growth, with this approach, is not to demonize anyone you had had trouble with before the session. No Judgment – no anger – no coercion while in the Magical Conversation space together.

Your Pot of Gold at the end of the Rainbow

You walk into a room, your eyes meet, you connect, you click! There is a spark of *inner* recognition and connection with love, with friendship, even with colleagues and clients. There might be 100 people in the room, there might be 10, but the number is irrelevant. It is the fact that there are men and women around or near you. Some will glide past you without notice and without acknowledging you. Others may nod or greet you briefly out of little more than politeness. Still, others may stop and chat or engage in a lengthier conversation.

As you walk down a street or enter a building or board an elevator, you are able (if you choose) to connect with people. It is the experience and the feeling that matters more than the content.

An anonymous quote says, "There are no such things as strangers, only friends you haven't met yet." The point is, you are virtually surrounded by hundreds or thousands of people, especially if you work in a city, run your own businesses, and even live quietly in suburban neighborhood. Whether on social media or face-to-face, use the same guidelines shared here. You are acquainted with many, several on a first name basis, and a number more intimately as friends and family. There is no shortage of people in your world… people that, should you choose to, you can get to know better. Why is it you will connect with some and not with others? Is it magic?

"Believe in love and harmonize your message using your heart-center, not your head logic"

For me, those are magic words. It is your heart, not head that will take you to the final stages of success regarding the personal outcome of your Magical Conversations. How you make the magic mix work for you with people you attract to your conversation space is 5% luck, and 95% your heart intention and good practice if you wish to become a magnet for your and other's happiness.

I consider that using positive heart-centered words and actions, sharing with loving intention is the only way to tune into those different from you. A successful relationship is always possible if you know why you are who you are, and that the magic, and it is real, exists in love, not fear. My core wisdom is that love strengthens all that is good in my world. Simple? Common sense? You need to decide, having read this far, why you choose love over fear, why you trust in *yourself,* and whether you believe that holding loving intentions for many people in today's world is possible for you in business as well as in life.

The loving intentions I hold dear and have experienced in my own life to overcome fear, sadness, and conflict, were revealed through facing the unknown, experiencing the flow, and at least taking a swing at the curve balls thrown at me. Knowing that I start my value with 'me' and not in a selfish fashion, the "I am OK being me" in a truly selfless manner. Being 'me,' knowing 'you,' sharing us. Remember the value creation must flow.

While learning from my life lessons, I became responsible for knowingly, appropriately, and completely nourishing the companionship of others with care, trust, and respect that only comes when you commit yourself to practicing the values-principles I shared earlier.

A Magical Conversation Partnership

I'd like to share my personal role models for all I am and achieve today. I am truly blessed. I dedicated this book to my parents. Their story matters to me.

My parents lived a long, love-filled life that included a marriage of 62 years, from 1939 until my father passed away at age 91 in 2001. My mother's only love since age 21, she lived another 8 years after he passed away. Although always missing him, she loved her life. She loved life and her life defined love and friendship. She never stopped loving him and feeling his essence around her. At 93 she realized it was time to go to him. They both defined, for me, the magnificence and exquisite nature of loving each other unconditionally. It wasn't always perfect harmony I am sure, still their love for each other and their lives each day was unquestioned and an example to all who knew and loved them in return.

Their **Relational Quotient** was high and not only did their love ripple life around them, but it was also consistent and built on a well-practiced set of values-based principles, behaviors, words, thoughts, beliefs, and deeds.

Being with them from birth into my 60s was how I learned *The Power of Authentic Harmony.*

Over their lifetime, they experienced a world war, the industrial revolution, man on the moon, social change, and the start of the digital revolution, all while bearing and caring for 4 children, in a home large enough for visiting extended family. They always lived with eyes wide open, a compassionate heart, strong family values, and a joy for service to their friends and local community. They always noticed the rainbow.

One Saturday morning recently, I awoke with their memory and a picture in my mind.

My soulmate Jim and I were living in Kuala Lumpur at the time and had had one of those days prior where an obstacle had raised its head and we had fallen out badly. A sign that loving intentions are present in your conversations is when such an occurrence comes without you losing sight of the rainbow. That was my waking thought. Instead of going to the trash can and throwing your life away, take heed that these moments are precious gifts. I started to draw. I drew a colored rainbow under which there were grey clouds.

As I imagined the best Magical Conversation, I desired to resolve our issues that Saturday, I recognized that it takes sunshine and rain to create magical colors, the whole spectrum from red to orange, yellow, green, blue, indigo, and violet. Interestingly, Jim, who is a musician, recalled a song recorded by the Oak Ridge Boys titled "It Takes a Little Rain." The lyrics of the chorus were: "It takes a little rain, to make love grow… it's a heartache and the pain… that makes a real heart show… if the sun always shines… there's a desert below… it takes a little rain… to make love grow."

In the rain clouds, you see the dark issues gathering strength. The wind huffs and puffs and blows hot and cold (depending on which climate you're in) and then you get stuck in the *stuff of life*.

As I expressed this to Jim that morning, in my drawing, we realized that when we got stuck in stuff, we were arguing in the dark clouds and rain and letting in the despair. As we refocused, we recognized the issues were less relevant when we stood together and felt the rainbow's energy surround and lift us. My advice that day was that we set intentions to recognize when stuff got in the way. This did not mean that he and I could not tackle issues. It did, however, give us a space to speak our truth and not be offended; to listen with an embracing heart even with tough topics!

The clouds can contain issues, major or minor. Those listed in my drawing were commonplace topics such as money, trust, friends, family, relationships, interdependence, and intimacy in love, differences, and perspectives on business and life.

Yours may be personal to your intimate life situation, but the process is the same in business boardrooms as well as around the family dinner table. Recognize when it's a cloud and do not destroy your rainbow. We found our pot of gold that morning and ever since when challenges arise.

Remember the lighthouse message at the beginning of this book, it is an image that is central to my work with Corporate Heart International. The lighthouse was my parents shining their light for me to flow safely through my often-rough seas. They taught me about the rainbow seen from their lighthouse so I could find my safe journey especially when unexpected waves rolled.

We run this Lighthouse exercise with client teams to explore what 'stuff of life' arguments, tensions and misunderstandings deplete team performance. When colleagues are distracted and stressed, it impacts many aspects of engagement, performance, and creativity. Through the Magical Conversations series, the collective intentions in each team's rainbow grow colorful seeds to flower great results that everyone is proud to own. This is a creative way to resolve with collective wisdom.

It takes a few sessions to participate in no-judgment awareness, sharing experiences in safety, listening without ego, opens people to share in ways they never imagined before. I am always so excited to set client companies on this journey of collective wisdom and self-discovery together.

There are many times in everyday home life, especially with home working and hybrid working today where this approach is even more important. Technology has changed the nature of work: we find life and business merged today. You may get caught in the *stuff of business*; the deal, the money, the operations, the control, the pressure to win. Business becomes fragile when *stuff* takes precedence over people and feelings. Even when the business is robust, bad relationships and dysfunctional conversations can make or break a deal or undermine large operations. When you build Magical Conversations into the culture of your business, you and those around you will bring forth the best results.

This approach helps individuals with work relationship difficulties as well. I was coaching a senior male client in British Telecoms, in the UK, who had presentation nerves. A shy man and 6 foot 4 inches tall, he would present as a willow tree, bending to the wind. The truth was his female boss was a tornado and he was intimidated by her demands. Helping him to be aware of this GDI© archetype, he discovered that he was a feminine-minded gentle *Philosopher*, and she was a tough masculine-minded female *Magician*.

My client gained an insight into how to deal with her. As she demanded his attention on a project, he would ask her for the deadline and negotiate for time. He managed her *instructional* approach, by *asking* for time rather than hiding away. She knew he was dependable, accurate, and would perform; and had previously doubted his command and decision-making. Once they came to this understanding, she would head off to her next meeting feeling confident in his work.

upshot was that they became best colleagues and had many more Magical Conversations to form a friendship working relationship.

He remarked to me on our exit interview that he now understood her and him. The core reason I was brought in to manage had melted away and his confidence made him stand head and shoulders above his colleagues quite literally!

RECAP 4Rs

Your **RELATE-ability** is the natural evolution of your own grounded *sense of self as* key as you enter each Magical Conversation with loving intent. Your goal is to dissolve stuff and not get caught up in the rainstorm.

As we **REACT,** take **RESPONSIBILITY,** and recognize the **RISK** that is in front of us, we can enter these conversations and make the outcome right for all parties.

The major challenge in developing your practice of Magical Conversation is to let go of the past. The burden of the past can ruin your future success. To take **RESPONSIBILITY** is to practice letting go of negative history that often blocks the growth of your relationships. Holding on makes you weary. Sense the loving intention in every connection, relationship, and deal, especially when negotiating deals and or talking over money or intimacy.

The lessons learned already, however long you've been building a connection with someone, mount up like compound interest to trust and understand each other.

With *What's in Your Rainbow?* Exercise focuses on a person's ability to recognize what is urgent and/or important and what is 'stuff' to sort out rather than let it scupper your relationship.

To ensure that this exercise works for you (and your team) embrace a daily practice:

The daily practice of the Nine Values-Principles:

Speak with Authenticity - be yourself, do not wear a mask, every situation has two sides - an inside and an outside as well as your side and his/her/their side. Indeed, none of them are real. All perceptions are real to the perceiver.

Develop Trust & respect: whatever the distress points are, you are human, have feelings, your presence even in an argument needs respect. Only through naming your issue and seeking honesty and integrity in response, can you build trust.

Seek Empathy: listen to their views genuinely and mindfully. No assumptions. No battles. Seek understanding through mutually respectful words.

Notice Balance: sense the ebb and flow of any issue. Seek to place it in the bigger context of your mutual world and the world at large.

Check Perceptions: each is personal, and yours is real but not necessarily for the other person. All is perceived by the beholder.

Invite Perspectives: there can be many perspectives on any one issue. No one is right or wrong. It's dangerous territory to get into "I'm Right, you're wrong" and it has never won any mutuality contests! Honor other perspectives and thank them. You don't have to own them.

Disclose with Transparency: see through to the other person's heart logic alongside head logic. Share your vulnerability, your natural response to each issue topic generally and from your point of view. Do not attack but do not be walked over.

Establish Clarity: think and reflect on words used, body language, touch and pause. Notice if your message is received well by looking for positive signs, verbal and non-verbal. Do not plead or beg; do not control or push your views on others. State your needs and expectations slowly and calmly, then pause and take a deep breath. Feel the energy in the space between you and others.

Value Compatibility: use the natural flow of loving intentions to seek compatibility, not sameness. Herein magic is created. If dark clouds gather, hold firm to the compatibility you have been practicing and seek to complement the relationship you are building with another. Check in regularly to see that what you believe makes you compatible is what the other parties recognize too.

Practice, practice, practice

Remember your ultimate vision is a commitment to Magical Conversations without demands, yet, after an appropriate agreed time, with mutually beneficial actions to be taken. Be sharing and caring, value inter-dependence as the best healthy option, enjoy dynamic joy and disruptive abundance, seek joy overcoming fear, be sure of your own mind, body, and heart. You can win-win every time, even when not agreeing. You agree to disagree but walk away without anger. I practice these principles every day.

Do I always get it right? NO! Do I do my best? YES.

Find your own practices that ground your soul and your belief in your intentions to create a safe space of magic. Believe the unbelievable – it occurs in front of your eyes.

My practices have developed over many decades and taught me that if, in my heart, I can say "I'm sorry, forgive me and thank you, I love you" then I find peace and grounded calmness in any situation that might throw me a curved ball!

This is from a long-established Hawaiian mantra called **Ho'oponopono** - give thanks, talk of love, be sorry, and forgive. This simple yet effective recital has healed deep wounds of rejection, even illness. It comes from the Hawaiian Tribes who believe that this mantra or chant will heal their forefathers.

Look for your daily support practices as there are many. Find ones that suit you.

These apply to all aspects of life, business and personal. It may be meditation, breathing exercises, a class or therapy session, a walk in the park, or a stroll along the beach. Be kind to yourself as you would be to others.

My passion for being a mediator and seeker of authentic harmony has led me to understand that reactive judgments and anger make mutual resolution and happiness very hard to achieve. Over my lifetime of good experiences and some big hard-knock moments, I discovered that my desire to create harmony, even in sad, angry, or distressed moments, was about my inner desire for myself as well as the other person/people involved.

Random acts of kindness and showering the world with smiles just for the sake of happiness have been ideas that truly appealed to me all my life.

A Magical Conversation Launched My Life's Adventure

The morning of November 24th, 2011, I sat opposite a new acquaintance, James Omps, at a conference breakfast in Budapest, we had met the day before at the conference we attended and had caught that spark of connection that I mentioned earlier. We chatted much of the day as we watched the speakers perform. It was, however, the next morning we had a 35-minute magical conversation. Why did this occur?

A. The fact that he was sitting in that corner table was orchestrated by powers beyond our understanding.
B. He was just finishing his meal and was about to leave had I not arrived.
C. I had set and written intentions to meet my soulmate in my private journals, over the 16 years following my divorce.

To this end, I was always ready to make the most of any opportunity to meet and converse with someone if I even had an inkling that my soul mate might appear right there in front of me at any moment.

Timing was key. The attraction was there.

We had spent the day before, during the initial joint session in the main body of the conference, chatting and sparking off regarding work and potential business ideas. As a masculine-minded businesswoman and *Magician,* I love to talk about and create potential business deals.

The chit-chat the previous day with a newfound friend, Jim, who I perceived to be *Philosopher* in nature, was welcome. It had been an exhausting conference schedule. This breakfast meeting was different. 35 minutes over eggs and bacon, we explored the far reaches of the universe, from galaxy to galaxy and back again. We shared more deeply than most male-female first-meeting experiences.

I found myself joyful, transparent, and genuinely engaged, telling him things that people don't usually share. We shared values, passions, legacy visions, stories of families, and even talk of aliens and time travel too. We talked of sadness and separation; he shared the fact that his current wife had packed up and left him a month prior. He also talked with fondness about his long-term previous marriage relationship of 37 years to the mother of his 5 children. As we talked, he told me stories he had never shared with a stranger.

I recounted my divorce 16 years earlier, my ex-husband's steady decline in health, my grown-up children and grandchildren, and my enduring sadness over the loss of my mother who had died suddenly in the summer of the year. I was touched by the fact that, upon my return to England, I was destined to become a nomad within a week as I had to leave my flat share. I also mentioned that, while I was not overly concerned, my situation was causing quite a stir among my adult children, and I was unsure how to deal with that.

It was an extraordinary choice point in my life and there was this handsome loving man, single and in tune with me, sitting with blue eyes twinkling as he smiled at my every word in tune!

I didn't think any further than this was truly a Magical Conversation and so I shared my ideas on this concept and why it worked with him. He was intrigued. I was used to connecting with businessmen and women with ease, seeing men as friends and just like me, a businessperson. This time, however, it was more than that… much deeper and more personal than normal. It was not a 'chat up' session either.

He is Jim, my husband now, and is a gentle *feminine*-minded introvert creative *Philosopher*, one of my GDI© Archetypes type that appealed to me as a counterbalance to my *Magician masculine*-minded femaleness. As I came to know in our relationship, shared later that he had been stunned at how easy it was to talk to me about some challenging issues for him. He had had cancer, had chemo, and radiation therapy, and nearly died, but survived. He felt safe to share and I was honored to be that space holder. Kindness, compassion, empathy, and willingness to hear another's story were my mantra for life. It was the right place, the best space, I was ready. Trust in yourself, that you are worthy and that your *Magical Love Conversation* may turn up at any time. Just be ready!!

I didn't foresee at that moment that within a year we'd be married Oct 7th, 2012, and we would then go and live in Malaysia for 4 years, on a different continent, Asia-Pacific until 2018. After this, we spent a year in California, and now live in Nevada. The USA is a new continent for me as a green card resident. I didn't know, nor did he, that we would be where we are today, sharing the adventure of a lifetime, launching this book first in January 2019; and now reprinting this updated edition in 2022 after two years of a pandemic that has changed our world and yours! We never imagined the world we experience now online, venturing onto live conferences and online programs, and building the power to ensure that legacy we spoke of that time in the magical conversation breakfast of November 2011.

We are ready to change the world if the world is ready to listen.

Our legacy statement was then and is now "to leave the world a better place for having been here" a world that knows *The Power of Authentic Harmony* and a Magical Conversation formula to share all topics even the most challenging ones that seem off the agenda. All is possible with the intentions set and the vision grounded in our lighthouse.

Was I a stranger that morning? Was he? We shared the feeling that we had known each other forever… in another place or another time? There was no intimacy, no kiss, merely the joy of connection, considerable fun, and genuine laughter as we sat through the morning's conference program.

Three hours later, we exchanged business cards shortly before I left for the airport. Then, a wistful goodbye, a soft, reassuring squeeze of the arm and a goodbye peck on the cheek, a professional farewell, and a spoken promise to one day work together. I walked away wondering how that could transpire. London… Las Vegas? That is a very long commute!!!

After 6 months and 45,000 words in emails between us, we had gotten to know more about each other and eventually confessed our growing love for one another. I flew to Las Vegas on May 21, 2012. Our first kiss confirmed that I had met my soulmate.

Has the journey been smooth? No. Exciting? Yes. Rewarding? Definitely.

I share my story to share that when you are prepared to attract Magical Conversations and seek to use *The Power of Authentic Harmony*, rather than anything negative and controlling, you can flow to the greatest happiness and abundant success. Through my practice, I have gained a new awareness of how Magical Conversations can help us grow in prosperity, not merely wealth but life's legacy of love and happiness too.

Understanding Jim's ill health after surgery, our residing in a new country, with our new and growing relationship, an irregular cash flow, relatively high cost, using our wits, and finding work, this adventure has been challenging and rewarding and a tale to share in another book maybe? Life is all about possibilities and choices, values and beliefs that can change your journey of understanding, and new habits that can form if you decide to allow loving intentions and Magical Conversations to work for you as a choice for your life.

A Formula for Our Successful Magical Conversation:
---

1. **No Judgment, No Anger, No Coercion of over-controlling words or behaviors**
2. **Be Open-minded, Joyful, Mindful, and Flowing**
3. **Come from your heart not your head (listen and share in alignment with your experiences of life)**
4. **Set the intention to raise your consciousness to allow transformation in your life.**
5. **Together use the space and time to seed possibilities and opportunities and watch as your world transforms.**

Developing Magical Conversations into a way of life for personal and professional goals has helped me to raise my message, monetize my connections, and fulfill my mission for a conscious loving authentic harmonious world. Now I share this formula with you, one that I know will transform your business and your life. You can 'pull' success to you rather than 'push' to sell yourself. Make way for magic and the harmonic pull of prosperity and happiness.

This is how I have evolved the Magical Conversations formula as an intentional strategy for life and for business. It's one part Pure Magic and three parts learning, practicing, and living the 9 Values-Principles set out here. It's all about bringing something of yourself to a conversation; something that comes from your heart and is moderated by the mind. Your truth is important when words and deeds align. The experience of YOU with others is key. Once you have prepared yourself as described throughout this book, you have set your loving intentions and got to know yourself, then you are ready to proceed.

Invite people to a Magical Conversation (officially)

Magical Conversations can be an organized gathering or an instantaneous meet-up with family and friends. I ran Magical Conversation Circles for over eight years in the UK and four years in Malaysia. The organized circles are time-bound (3 hours maximum; enough to seed amazing creativity), and contributors are invited. The *rules* apply in all situations, nonjudgment, no anger, no coercion. The outcomes are creative thoughts, ideas, learning, shifting perspectives, knowledge, imagination sparks and practical solutions found that can be acted on later. The topic in the middle of the table is the focus, not the personalities or what people do, it's what they can give to the conversation that creates what matters. Experiences shared will lead us to learn about others, joyful sharing brings love and happiness into the experience. Curiously, the focus is the topic, not the people, however, the results enhance all engagement even if each takes away a different memory. Remember it is the experience and the feeling that you will enjoy as much as the content. In practice, invite someone to make notes in a mind-mapping style or use Post-it notes to jot down ideas and words in a random collation. This serves as a pictorial reminder and not a 'to-do' list!

This works for personal conversations.

* Decide which topic is to be discussed, start with the positive rainbow intentions especially if dealing with the *stuff of life* - your clouds.
* Ensure your vehicle (your body, mind, and heart) is valuable to you and make sure you have the best fuel in your engine and, where possible, arrange the best time for the other person/s to be in the conversation.
* Be in the right mind frame, breathe and inhale loving thoughts before commencing.
* Ensure you create a loving space, light airy, sit side by side, or opposite each other, in a comfortable at ease manner, in a circle

if you have choice. If the physical environment is challenged by *stuff*, then do your best to create a *safe* space to talk.

❖ Eliminate as many noises and distractions as possible. Make sure the other/s in your conversational space are well and make them feel safe to contribute.

Ensure all parties hear and are clear of the *rules*.

A. State that there are *No Judgments* allowed and invite all to avoid assumptions.

B. Encourage an open mind and a values-based conversation.

C. State your values simply in your welcome, appropriately. For example, "it is a pleasure to be here, let's share our experiences and value our differences in a mindful manner with respect for all."

D. Add descriptors appropriate to your goals. Is it a serious topic, a creative exploration, a personal issue, or a business process? It may be any topic, the *rules* apply.

E. Use your own experiences and viewpoints and share with authenticity and clarity.

F. Set your standards consistently.

G. Invite your perspective to be respected as your unique perceptions of any situation.

H. At the same time respect other's perspectives as theirs. Be open-minded.

By engaging in this way, we honor each other and especially our different behavior dynamics as men and women, of different generations, cultures, and sexual orientations.

Aim to understand all who enter the space you create and allow others to share within your welcome. Your objective is to guide not control.

Do set a time dimension appropriately so you can manage the contribution timeline before any actions need to occur. Actions come after the Magical Conversation has closed and everyone has left the room for a break.

Speak *Without Anger* or any meanness; breathe deeply before you start, enroll his or her attention, set these intentions and honor all parties. Bring mindful joy and energy to the space you all share and the words that are beginning to flow.

Preparation is key.

1) Prepare your mind, heart, and body before you start. Breathe in with your values e.g., *love trust honor*. Think, experience, and be open-hearted in your intention. Share your experiences not opinions.
2) Settle your body into a mindful state. Keep loving memories in your heart and recognize the emotional bank balance you have created over your life. Take care with your body language and lean in to listen.
3) Listen, listen, listen, and then speak to first check your understanding when offered the opportunity. Speak from your heart, spare lovingly and consciously. Do not interrupt or start until sure the space between you holds your mutual loving intentions.

Finally, do not allow *Coercion or Controlling Actions*. This is a safe space; so, there is no overt pressure or urgency to decide or draw a conclusion until all is ready and the session is closed. Don't make promises you might not be able to keep.

Respect time and pressure influence: Do not put a control or any urgency such as "you must…" command into any conversation you wish to be magical. This will affect the flow.

Observe Diversity and Gender Dynamics in the Room

Before and during the Magical Conversation itself, be aware of the different perspectives that people bring with them i.e., their *GDI*©️ *Archetypes* plus their generational experiences, their sexual orientation, their abilities or impairments and their cultural and ethnic history.

Diversity is a vital essence in this magic mix and needs careful consideration in every conversation.

Carefully note the fundamental differences between men and women as a starter. This is my major focus in collaborating with clients. We have shared the four natural *GDI*© *Archetypes* and their attributes in conversation styles. I have mentioned these throughout this book, now we explore further and introduce a map that shines a light on this circle of life's conversations.

Men tend to converse in *boxes* one topic at a time, with a task-focused linear approach. This *"either or"* style can bring a limit to a free flow conversation while women converse in *circles*, multi-tasking, nurturing, and 'feeling' their way to relationships and results. This is what I call an *"and - and"* approach to conversations.

Within each gender biology, there is a range of *positive masculine* to *positive feminine* traits that occur and can be witnessed in different behavioral approaches to conversations. Remember my masculine mind in my female body? My natural conversation style is grounded in my female nature, i.e., *circular* and *relationship* focused, however my mindset is logical, thinking, task focused and seeking collaboration for solutions required. This latter style is more *boxed* straight-line, masculine, in process. My conversation style will go to the extreme of my logic preference especially in stress and under pressure; and will go this preference also to employ the best of my *positive masculine* behavior, looking for facts and not feelings, and may be received as over direct and male (but I am not a male!) Men and women range in conversational style along a *positive masculine– positive feminine* axis within each gender's biology/physicality, in addition to *male and female* biological preferences influencing their reactions and conversation styles.

These *GDI*© *Archetypes* are not personalities or gender identities. Whichever identity you choose will impact the dynamics in every conversation and situation.

I'm a Masculine-minded Female, I call this MF a *Magician* My husband Jim, is a gentle intuitive male, a Feminine-minded Male FM, *Philosopher*, a thinker-feeler.

Men range from this archetypal baseline to a more Masculine-minded Male MM, action *Ruler* man style. Women range in style from mine, *Magician* to a more Feminine-minded female FF, *Sovereign* - more detailed focused, verbally dexterous, kinesthetic, and intuitive. In studying my own style and physicality during the last 30 years, I observed that our body skeleton and stance also played a part in our presence and demeanor.

These observations led me to understand and create a 360° perspective to include a baseline using the two-dimensional biological divide '*male–female*' axis as I realized we all need to value the core energy driver of the '*positive masculine – positive feminine*' axis. Physicality, body shape, stance, left-right brain, and behavioral reactive traits are added to form a complete circle of life's conversations.

The map goes deeper into the application of factors already known from writers such as Dr John Gray "Men are from Mars, Women Are from Venus" in which he writes similarly of the two core territories you see in my GDI© Archetypes illustrated here, the *boxed area* (male Mars) and the *circular territory* (female Venus) are visuals to help you recognize core differences.

The additional drill-down in my studies, born from my own experiences and observations of 100s of men and women over last 20 years, is that physicality (bone structure and stance) shows an alignment to potential behavioral characteristics. The straighter the structure of the body, and the more angular the features, the more likely the male or female with those features will use *masculine* style behaviors such as *logic, processing, thinking, linear thinking*. Like myself, in my own straight stance and skeleton, I knew I was female yet not as *feminine* as many females I knew. Likewise, softer bone structures and stance indicated *feminine* behaviors, softer approaches, *e.g., more intuitive traits and verbal dexterity*. These traits are not indicators of sexual orientation at all. It merely allows females to have a *masculine-minded logical approach to life* and males to have a *feminine-minded intuitive approach to life*. Every sexual orientation, LBGT is on the map and the dynamics that occur for all human beings as they relate to others. If you are a male, you are in the range MM-M -FM, if a female, in the range MF-F-FF in a 360° perspective. If T(Trans) then you may move across from M-F, or F-M.

My years in business have helped me understand these ranges and design these **GDI© Archetypes** to apply to every situation where people relate to each other. This map enables you to navigate a diverse group of styles when you are in conversation. I have worked with this map with hundreds of clients to start their awareness conversation not to label them. Knowing where you start, who's around your table, and what communication route to take with other types aids your best chances for magnetic Magical Conversations.

For ease of understanding the basic conversational differences, be aware that men chatter less and work systematically in defined topic *boxes and straight-line communication*, one topic at a time. Women flow in *circles* of conversation and tangential yet intertwined messages often happening at the same time in a tapestry of thinking and feeling.

Women tend to ask questions without always needing answers – it. way to explore feelings *and* facts - while men tend to ask questions to complete tasks 'yes/no' and hear questions as tasks to be resolved.

When located on the GDI MAP, each woman and man can decide how they wish to navigate relationships from their chosen preference/location in the style that best suits their authentic self.

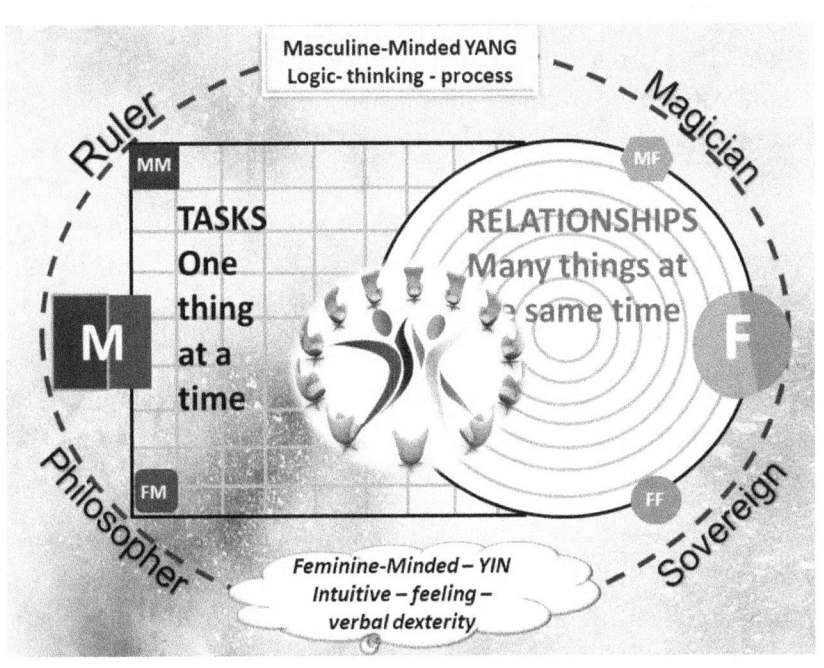

GENDER DYNAMICS INTELLIGENCE© MAP 2024

Here are a few GDI© observations to be aware of as you engage in Magical Conversations.

Men Be Aware: women need to have time to state their feelings over and over, circular in nature. When they ask questions, they do not need a solution too quickly even if they are asking for one. Use positive affirmations, repeat any compliments honestly, hold an appreciative gaze, and remember she is NOT in a box.

She enjoys being able to tend or befriend. She cares, that is why an issue you see in the cloud, she may see in the rainbow. Some women may be more likely to be logical (MF) and get challenging, responding with an energy that appears to say, "I can do without you." Some on the other hand, may turn inward if you're insensitive and disappear into feelings (FF). Females often like to get things off their chest and once delivered feel better, while if the man is drowning emotionally, he may not ask for a lifeline!

Women Be Aware: men cannot often take too much chatter and emotion without being stranded in their "either/or" solution-focused BOX.

Men may want to bring a solution to you if you appear distressed especially if they feel they are the cause of your distress. He wants to help and if he cannot find a solution that he believes is right for you, it's a painful void to be avoided. If he feels attacked and you feel like crying, your emotions drown him like a river torrent. He *receives* it like a tornado of anguish and does not know how to quell it. He fights with justification anger *or* flights out the door! The MM nature may get impatient with you and the FM may disappear into his cave or computer!

Men often talk about topics, like work, money, sex, cars, sports, music, romance, family, retirement, etc., but often they don't mix them as women intertwine topics and the meaning of life.

Yin & Yang

The conversational balance is in your hands. Male, female, masculine, feminine, etc., all differences may become blessings.

8

Harmonize Your Message and Find Success

YOUR Pot of Gold is at The End of YOUR Rainbow...

The rainbow is where your mutual intentions live and which you can declare and share with others and come alive in a Magical Conversation session. Set personal intentions to be magical within yourself before entering the conversation. Do share and agree on the rules openly with others so they own the mutuality too. For a business as in life success, the same rules and loving intentions, principles and assessments as laid out in this book, apply.

Make sure you value yourself, your practice of knowing YOU is maximized by following the guidelines and principles in this book. Ensure *The Value Creation Cycle* evolves from your heart center, not your head logic. Keep your Relational Quotient in top form, with daily workouts as you understand your 4Rs and study others who are different to you. Be OK with behavioral and conversational differences; therein springs the magic fusion!

Know your Passion, Communication Choices, Assets and Vulnerabilities. Add them all to your personal growth plans and know them deep within you. You are now a walking-talking harmony magnet and ready for action.

As you attract or repel depending on how YOU relate and tune into others, recognize you own *The Power of Authentic Harmony*. In today's marketplace, relationships matter highly. The power once switched on stays strong. As you practice the loving intention of this Magical Conversation style of communication, you will be ready to bond not only with family and friends and your intimate soulmate, but you can also attract clients and business deals to enhance your prosperity.

If you run your own business, careful and consistent development of your *Value Creation Cycle*, and devote time to the lessons in this book, will add to your winning credentials in whatever service you offer. You're ready to monetize your conversations for a deal, a sale, a joint venture, or a long-term prosperity partnership by not pushing but *pulling*. Switch on the power and follow the rules, and people will enjoy being connected to you and the empowerment of your authentic harmonious presence.

It may be that you are an employee on a rising career path, but YOUR understanding of what is occurring around you as you lead conversations at team meetings or in the boardroom matters for your success. Watch the chatter in the corridors of your workspace and develop your profile as a Magical Conversations enthusiastic employee and you will get noticed – for the right reasons. In business, shared dialogue and rapport building are critical attributes as you rise through the organization. Today there are many challenges in the workplace where men and women sometimes battle for power, you can become the magnet for a new way to converse that others may not have experienced.

You may be the leader, the boss, male or female, who wants to inspire a mixed management team of men and women and create the best culture that embraces all parties. Other diverse factors make up your workforce and Magical Conversation Circle events are an ideal way to bring often delicate or contentious issues into a safe zone. By following the rules, the magic works as everyone shares without judgment, anger, or controls. I have run such sessions and am always very grateful for the creative content that arises. My intention is to create the right space, to adhere to the rules, and to allow human beings to feel the natural wisdom that arises.

Set loving intentions in the workplace and experience the impact you can have on the right people, those who like you seek authentic harmony. Many people need to be heard and often are fearful to speak. Help them expand their confidence to share and grow. As the rules become a natural part of people's lives, with loving intentions as the magic wand, difficult subjects and situations can be overcome.

I have worked to resolve tricky situations with business clients. My remit is to sort out 'bad behavior'. This is particularly acute with the current climate of sexual harassment cases being a lurking threat. CEOs need to develop mixed diverse cultures when differences are honored, and inappropriate behavior by staff reprimanded. The goal is to develop a mutually owned moral compass. I experience diverse client cultures dealing with these issues. In my experience with clients, it is the unspoken fear that harm happens when boundaries are crossed often unconsciously. The turnaround comes when people realize that they are all engaged in creating a new culture of healthy collaborative working.

Collective ownership of a workplace culture is key to collaboration, the leaders may set the product or service values for the company, but a wise leader engages his or her staff in owning these values in their hearts. My company is called Corporate Heart International and focuses on the heart matters of business consciousness; it delivers programs and products that ensure the heart of every employee is engaged. When the heartfelt values of a business resonate with its employee's healthy performance, from leaders to front-line staff, then productivity through collective performance increases.

Let me give you an example. I designed a major engagement program for a car distributor network in the UK, the widespread nature of the network had made for a fragmented work ethos. Bringing staff together into Magical Conversation Circles and setting topics that built trust and respect was a powerful engagement process and enabled everyone to get involved. It shifted the energy of the business landscape for all parties, managers, mechanics, sales teams, and administration.

"The engagement sessions rolled out across the Express Fit Dealerships were brilliantly designed to capture the essence of the key message "Adding Value". We are required to shift the 'hearts and minds' of everyone delivering our 'Express Fit' service. I was personally amazed that such a short session can create a great deal of energy, honest sharing, and commitment to action ....and gave everyone a new sense of personal value within the business!" *Julie Rosser, Manager-Workshop Programs, Peugeot Express Fit dealership*

Bring your magic to work!

Observe who is around your circle, at your table, in your deal meetings. Are they the MM, male *Rulers*, bullet point action men, directive and structured? Are they FM, male *Philosophers* servant leaders, intuitive feelings-type men, great at keeping people onside? Are they MF, female *Magicians*, logic-driven, ideas, connections, and concepts led, in-their-head women? Are they FF, female *Sovereigns*, queens of their domains, detailed, creative, sensitive, and nurturing? Attracting, connecting, and building relationships with all types is the best way to gain faithful clients, customers, a community, and a loyal tribe.

Make sure 70% plus of your words and actions in any exchange are positive and embrace each person engaged. Then factor in your wisdom to manage the 30% that is the unknown, the challenging or confusing. You are building the rapport to make issues easier to work through. Know when to listen and when to speak. The results you desire will emerge as you flow together, and you realize the rainbow intentions that overarch throughout the initial engagement process of shared experiences and the continued Magical Conversations you practice in the lifetime of every relationship.

Remember to connect at a heart-center level first (not head), communicate based on the principles we have covered, and create conversations that flow, engaging everyone's styles and diversity factors. You are the host of your own Magical Conversations so set the scene, build the atmosphere, and guide others without them knowing, embrace loving intentions and the experience you create will bring the results you desire.

Here is a summary list to guide you as you become an expert at your own Magical Conversations.

Setting the Scene

1. Set intentions rather than expectations.
2. Guide the conscious unifying purpose of the conversation and honor all participants.
3. Decide the mutual topic/s and underlying scenario with consent and within the purpose as agreed.
4. Agree on core principles: no anger, no judgment, no urgency, pressure, or stress.
5. Define mindful goals with no overt persuasion to action unless organic and mutually agreed.
6. Give all permission to speak and observe core polite etiquette.
7. Create the best listening environment and respectful trust to all, sitting in a circle wherever available, using open space and clear desks where possible in work environments.
8. Facilitate an energy flow, time keeping and monitoring the space as safe and sacred to the conversation at hand.
9. Oversee the process without control, seeking inclusion and collaboration.
10. Where appropriate, charter the conversation output on paper, unattributed to any one person, and in a mind-map display.

The Results for You and Others and Your Business.

If you are creating an invitation for a scheduled Magical Conversation Circle and new parties are curious as to why this will benefit the participants, you might wish to share the following as potential reasons with individuals and groups.

These are the results that my clients have reported to me after the formal experience:

1. Getting your true voice heard without being rebuffed.
2. Being confident to share and learn at the same time.
3. Being unafraid to comment on sensitive and serious topics.
4. Enjoying the potential widening of perspectives and perceptions
5. Growing a far broader based knowledge of other's views
6. Gathering 'ah ha' awareness on any chosen variety of topics
7. Making connections and collaborations based on people's values, authenticity, and trust.
8. Furthering creative opportunities for business and life on a local and global scale

Bonus Results as you expand your Business Operations with a Magical Conversation Forum or Wisdom Circle

As a leader in your own business or in a corporation, you will find that the scheduling of formal sessions sets the scene for.

- Building a cohesive co-creative team
- Ensuring a more flexible inspirational leadership style
- Embedding a collaborative and empowered inclusive work culture.
- Seeding unexpected opportunities and ideas that bring profitability and sustainability.
- Smoother operational and professional relationships and cooperation among your people

At the end of the day, my experience is that people would rather live and work in a loving environment than one built on fear. People feel great when they feel their voice and contribution count, and when they do, they create better business results all around and profits grow exponentially!

This testimonial is from a major client in central London:

Pauline has a unique understanding of the differences in communication and thought patterns between men and women. She can add value to any business that aims to improve diversity, leverage women's talent, and develop a more productive workforce. She designed an inspirational workshop by interviewing three of the most senior women, and she was able to obtain from them very valuable feedback on how more junior employees can improve their careers.

Again, she demonstrated how men and women can engage better with each other by adapting their style to the masculine/feminine personality of the recipient. She also suggested the styles and words that we can use to obtain greater results when conveying important messages. Given the unique engagement with the audience, expertise, and value that she can add to a company, I have no hesitation in recommending Pauline to any company that wishes to improve the retention of women's talents. Thank you so much for all the magic you brought to my life!"

Giuliana Bruce, Barclays, London

I have personally designed and hosted many hundreds of Magical Conversations, for senior leaders, male and female, to explore and share their viewpoints, possibilities, and visions, enabling new solutions to emerge. This has been across the UK, Asia Pacific, and now the USA. The GDI© Archetypes are the science within the practice of Magical Conversations. The practice of all I have shared will light up *The Power of Authentic Harmony* and produce amazing results that ensure people work better so profits go up and costs go down.

The cultures that evolve will find fiscal results emerging e.g., reduced arbitration and less need for damage control mechanisms when people misbehave, or occupational health crises arise when inappropriate harassment causes disaster not just for company reputations but for people's lives.

The growth of a Magical Conversations culture is like refueling your car with high-octane *authentic harmony* gas. As I develop leaders and help them manage their 'gas', their lives, as well as their workforce, improve 100%, and the organizations they lead become more aware of the broader social issues and corporate social responsibility, setting new ethical guidelines and business etiquette, while connecting with community issues that surround their business.

The results of this approach to engagement through non-judgmental conversations are multiple and diverse - bright ideas, innovative products, and a collaborative consciousness to do good are only a few. As the culture engages everyone the gas ignites healthy high-impact performance and more productivity. The impact is felt as *the Power of Authentic Harmony* flows out from employees to customers and clients.

The Corporate Heart International vision is to help people and businesses to build conversations that matter and take actions that make a difference to people *and* profits. If we are going to create a new future, a future fueled by authentic harmony, the story starts now!

A few final notes from my own experience:

- First to be loving in your intentions, seek to understand others, build rapport with a high relational quotient, value differences, and create Magical Conversations that embrace all parties.
- Do not focus on money even though financial gain is the result.
- Focus on the relationship and the messages, the energy, and the connection.

These conversations will flow you into the unknown. Be ready for the unexpected deal, the contract that swells your bank balance, and an outcome that delivers an infinite range of possibilities that you never imagined. That is magic!

Welcome to your magic, have some serious fun and enjoy the journey. YOU are 'in charge' of YOU and the impact you can create in other people's lives and your own is in your hands.

"First, value and love your life so that you can impact others appropriately with loving intentions.... know others, know yourself. Magical Conversations is a practice to engage The Power of Authentic Harmony in all matters of the heart."   ... Dr Pauline Crawford

---

A pot of gold is at the end of YOUR rainbow. Set intentions and make welcome the magical conversations within you. Enjoy the journey to success.

PARABLE

Bears or Birds - Who's in Charge?

Can we create a Joint Custody World?

In the search for a new understanding among men and women, I write this story to tease your imagination. It is a parable, a simple story to illustrate what I sense are some of the barriers to creating a Joint Custody World with the principles laid out in The Power of Authentic Harmony.

I asked myself, can men and women come together, honoring their human uniqueness, seed the ground with nature's gifts and harvest new conversations that help everyone thrive equally. The outcomes projected – if parties so desire - would aim to resolve conflicts, regenerate new economies, and structure societies to embrace humanity, family life, health, wealth, and abundance of opportunities for all.

If women had been in charge over the last centuries would our today's world be different? We may never know. However, using knowledge, experience, and a wonderful dose of imagination, take a journey into this fantasy story of many possibilities using the unlikely metaphor of bears (men) and birds (women) to tackle a challenged business world and the economic chaos we experience today.

These two different species can entwine their two natures into one vision. This story is not so unlikely.

ONCE UPON A TIME ...

... "a business *city*" had been built over many decades on the "square mile" principle; every inch measurable and maximized for the owners, each square inch sold and resold, marked up, traded down; every skyscraper fielded a magnificent view, yet many streets were cold from the deep shadows the towers made. The inner streets were paved with gold and had a labyrinth of tunnel journeys and caves connected by long corridors, lift shafts, stairs and out of this a very hard-nosed culture had grown. This *City* was designed and inhabited by the Bears.

There was another *City* - known more as a "*community*"– hidden away over those same past decades. This was designed to be a community culture, with open landscapes, cozy rooms, and play stations for the younger members to learn and flourish, nesting nooks for conversations, space for innovation and creativity coffee breaks; here there were support systems that shared resources and reduced waste. This inner city was a mesh of inter-connected live wires and tree top nests. The Birds inhabited this inner *city*.

The Bears and the Birds were well known to each other as they had shared the earth together for millenniums, breathing the same air, drinking the same water, eating up the same resources; however, they needed different things, they had different biological needs, and even though they often held similar aspirations and dreams for their future, their perspectives on how that came to be where subtly different.

Their mutual challenge was to understand each other as the two cities grew side by side; business and life began to intertwine. Over decades of changing times, with viral changes, technology, and flexible ways of socializing; *working and living together* had become blended in style. Many top-level Bears observed their world was changing and surrounding market and social boundaries collapsing, evolving, and revolving in ever decreasing circles. Many natural and economic disasters challenged the very foundations of the world that both Bears *and* Birds loved. They now faced a world-in-crisis and obstacles that threatened to undermine life as previously known.

The Bears continued to prowl their Bear's **City** There were not interested in the other city for business. Some were greedy, gruff, grizzly, and dangerous. They were very strong, grounded, and fearless. Many were strong and proud of their mighty presence and not keen to welcome Birds into their territory. A few were very wise and open to sharing with the Birds as they recognized their talents. Young cub bears were learning from their elders and played tough games, while some were afraid of their own shadows and acted like teddy bears, warm and cuddly, keen to be with the Birds nurturing embrace.

The Birds were quite different to the Bears. They were designed across many variable types with plumes of many-colored feathers, bodies of different sizes and wing spans spread to glide and soar. Big or small; wild or tame; some flew in formation, others lived as family units, others fought their own battles, while many twittered happily over the garden wall. Yet all the Birds had one thing in common, their core nurturing emotionality and reproductive capabilities. They achieved tasks by managing their resources, colleagues, friends, and family. Plus, they loved to chatter and sing beautiful, creative songs. They took care of their young and whether they lived with a loving Bear or not, they tended to their families, old and young.

Their major challenge in a world designed by the Bears was that once they were attacked, damaged, or caught on the ground or threatened, the Birds were terrified. Losing a limb, a wing, or a feather made them victims.

Increasingly the Birds learned to adapt to business, managing major responsibilities and leadership roles. Many decided to create their own enterprises and balance their lives appropriately. In doing this, the empowered Birds became noticed and even feared by Bears. The Birds swooped and soared; when they gained a love for power, they too preyed on the most vulnerable, pretending they were like Bears.

Many Birds flew on their own wings, expanding their remit to own their ideas.

It seemed that when Birds sang from their hearts and filled the sweet evening song of common sense, the sound of their voices infiltrated the airwaves of business and life for the better. They demanded inclusion and equality. Bears did not know what to do. As Birds left their nests to travel to and from work and home, they sought a work life balance that was alien to many Bears, yet they grew in numbers as the scent of financial independence made them flutter and flourish.

As the decades changed the nature of business and it impacted the family zone, Birds desire to be more and the Bears became defensive. They did not want Birds fluttering up the boardroom! Could the Birds seriously to be "in charge" of the Bears? This seems preposterous! (Bears said!!)

Increasingly the Birds started invading the Bear's *City* (where the Bears had regularly inhabited for their daily work) seeking bigger worms and prospects for their life's survival. They realized there were rich pickings for them too. It was tough going for the Birds to begin with as the Bears were big and strong. They had built their Bear's *City* to be the powerhouse that generated wealth and provided resources for their own caves. Their traditions were well embedded in their mind-set. They liked to end their day in the cosy nest of home loving Birds. They did not always approve of working Birds. They made it a perilous journey for many working Birds, who tried to perch on the higher levels of the skyscrapers, looking for safe habitats and life-saving deals.

As the truth dawned about the Birds desires to be in the Bear's *City*, many Bears did not want them in their workspaces and sharing their hard-earned stakes; however, the Birds were determined that they were there to stay and grew in numbers every year. The more conscious wise Birds and Bears knew that, for the survival of their world, the only way forward would be together.

The Bears could not understand why the Birds talked in circles, chattered with others, and used random tangents to think through problems. Bears thought and acted in boxes, directed in straight lines, and expected solutions to every question. The Birds longed to bring their circular birdsong to be truly valued and honored by the Bears as an intrinsic and valuable part of a fulfilled and successful work-life balance. They valued the Bears for their strength, tenacity, logical thinking, and especially their ability to be the major provider to the family. The Birds loved the adoration that the Bears gave them at home and in many communities where they nurtured their families of young Bears and Birds.

Once the working Birds discovered the Bear's *City* operations and financial criteria, they wanted a bigger piece of the pie. They knew they could add value, natural skills, more emotional intelligence, good relationship management, and different consumer knowledge to that which the Bears had. They knew they could deliver much of what the Bears offered yet with a nurturing inclusive spirit that would sustain better long-term results, combining a healthier lifestyle alongside traditional fiscal success. Yet given all that the Birds brought to the Bear's *City*, the gateways to the high skyscrapers often proved difficult and had closed combination locks that barred the doorways to the boardroom.

Can the Bears and the Birds sing a new Authentic Harmony song together?

Now times have changed. The internet highway, global trade, business from your home, education for all, and entrepreneurship have all blossomed and the Birds are flourishing too and sing their beautiful songs and lyrics even more than ever. Their activities, especially the younger Y and X Gen, and now Millennium and Digital Bears *and* Birds are creating new cultures and different perspectives that are meaningful and inclusive.

Of course, increasingly wise Bears and Birds are getting together and writing tunes of collaboration with cords of harmony to soothe the noisy chaotic world. More evidence shows that sharing this song in a magical conversation space allows for mutual creativity to grow. Seeking to listen to the different perspectives that the Bears have about Birds, and vice versa, without judgment or anger or trying to control the outcomes based on the past, is a pathway to real-synergy leadership. Many Bears and Birds find the complement of Bears and Birds both joyful and productive.

All generations can add to the music in an authentic harmony with a full repertoire of new business. Still, some older more traditional Bears do not understand these songs. When they try to sing along, their deep voices threaten the very nature of the Bird song.

The Bears can often get stuck with their macho 'pow-wow' power groups and warrior sports games. However, the shift has come with a world after lockdown where many Bears learned to be emotional and true to life's healthy balance.

The Bears and the Birds may still seem at odds with each other yet, as in nature, there is also an intimate attraction between them. Love is the fuel of transformation and a counterpoint to the fear that often made the Bear City impenetrable. In truth, Bears and Birds love each other and have done so since the beginning of time. When the attraction flourishes, they form families to parent new generations of Birds and Bears. Indeed, they naturally complement each other.

POSTSCRIPT

Can the Bears genuinely let the Birds into their Bear's *City* in ways that truly meet the needs of both? Can the Birds persuade the Bears to get together and co-create a new *Joint Custody World* *City* domain that integrates business and life, economic revival, and social cohesion?

Can they indeed share and co-create a circular landscape that combines squares and circles, straight lines and curves, operational excellence and decisions made with instincts, mixing emotions and facts that improve economies and family union with human care?

This proposition requires all species, equal and different, to engage. It is time for the Birds to take this opportunity without prejudice and malice even for the unforgivable injustices that may occur. Can we heal the ills and abuse that the Birds have been through to arrive at this choice point time? Can the Bears be led to a new space that they didn't create originally and welcome the new narrative?

"BUSINESS BLISS, BOOM OR BUST?"

WILL BEAR-GROWL OR BIRD-SONG WIN?

ONLY TIME WILL TELL.

THE END OF THE STORY IS STILL BEING WRITTEN...

MAYBE MAGICAL CONVERSATIONS HOLD THE KEY TO OUR FUTURE POT OF AUTHENTIC HARMONY GOLD?

THE AUTHOR – DR PAULINE CRAWFORD

Dr. Pauline Crawford's career started over 30 years ago as a Designer and Originator of the Gender Dynamics Intelligence (GDI©) Map. Her visionary perspective has entered a new phase with the pandemic turning the world of work upside down. Her mission is to embed *The Power of Authentic Harmony* among leaders as a core principle for the best healthy mix of women and men co-creating new narratives and exploring growth opportunities together.

With more than 30 years of experience working in the business sectors of the U.K., Europe, Asia, and the U.S., Dr. Pauline is Chief Vision Officer of Corporate Heart International, President of WAVE, World Association of Visionary & Entreprenologists; President 2023-24 for Rotary Club of Global Impact, Chairperson, Permanent Commission for Social Issues and Women Entrepreneurs WUSME, World Union of Small and Medium Enterprises. She joined IUE as a Director in 2012 when she met and married Dr James A. Omps, the President of IUE, The International University of Entreprenology.

An author and international speaker, Dr. Crawford has been able to introduce her unique concepts and programs across different countries and cultures of the world, fostering a new leadership narrative that honors women as never before. She envisions a real-life synergy of the best learning practices from the past and a humanity-oriented visualization of the future for all-inclusive prosperity. Her vision is for *The Power of Authentic Harmony* between women and men as the major force for businesses to host a corporate heart!

The Conversation Game Changer, Gender Dynamics Intelligence Authority, Internationally Certified Entreprenologist PHD, Magical Conversations Host, Dr. Pauline's mission is to educate leaders in the benefits of understanding human nature and core behavior traits that influence conversations, relationships, and performance outcomes, impacting individuals and whole communities to flourish personally, professionally, and commercially. She collaborates with clients from all sectors and across the globe, bringing unique tools and techniques to help individuals gain a deeper understanding of why they are who they are. Now a resident of the US, Dr. Pauline focuses on entrepreneurs and corporates keen to create success through people with the objectives of real synergy, relational energy, and performance excellence.

Her enterprise, Corporate Heart International, founded in 1999 in the UK, has expanded around the world with her travels. Dr. Pauline's study of how business performance is impacted by relational pressures and human misunderstandings has given rise to her unique behavioral approach of 'value creation' to embed authentic harmony as a driver for sustainable profitable success. She has a vision of global happiness and harmony through the cooperation of women and men leading meaningful enterprises that are effective to people, planet, prosperity, and peace.

With an additional role as G100 Global Wing for #Authentic Harmony & Positive Masculinity and part of a global network of 100 #WomenLeaders, this has allowed her to meet her audacious mission to enable conversations across genders to contribute positively to the empowerment and inclusion of all with a spirit of equality and harmony, mitigating violence and discrimination against girls and women worldwide.

"As we seek opportunities to grow The Power of Authentic Harmony, we must be prepared for the unexpected, the magical, the imagination, and more to solve the issues that appear unsolvable. Human life is our responsibility to love."

Dr Pauline Crawford

PROGRAMS AVAILABLE

THE POWER OF AUTHENTIC HARMONY

Roundtable Breakthrough Wisdom Circles for Leaders

Are you a Leader who has the desire to tap into the creativity and innovation of your team to explore the most challenging issues of the business? This Magical Conversations Wisdom Circle will enable you to do just that. This project includes pre sessions to clarify the topic at hand and the key question format for the session. Then you let go and attend as a participant equal to everyone else. Magic works!

MEN OF THE FUTURE NOW

An exclusive program for professional men
You are the role model for the man of the future. Events are influencing and determining how a MAN will function in both professional and social environments. If you want to be ahead of the curve rather than working overtime to catch up, **Men of the Future** will give you the roadmap to take you from here to your future success with ease.

WOMEN OF SIGNIFICANCE TODAY

An exclusive program for professional women
The need for women to step forward is paramount but it is going to take more than boldness. Beginning with determined and designed, **Women of Significance** is going to take your female leadership of the highest order. This program provides a guide and support systems that you can use to chart your path to being one of those leaders, being a woman of significance.

REAL SYNERGY WORKING TOGETHER

Exclusively for people in top management

Are you ready to gain the business advantage in all business circles? If you are ready to navigate the winning team, this is your opportunity to get the map that can take you from Point A to Point B without wasting your time.

Collaboration using **GDI© Gender Intelligence© Archetypes Map** to unlock top level success.

HOSTING MAGICAL CONVERSATIONS & GDI© MASTERY PROGRAM

Become a Certified Magical Conversations Host with GDI© Mastery.

This is a Six-Step Online Interactive Program, including Video Recordings, Workbooks, Assignments Webinars and Zoom Coaching Sessions:
1-Value Creation, 2-GDI© Archetypes Intelligence
3-Relational Quotient, 4-Partnerships & Principles
5-Harmonize Your Business, 6-Business & Life Growth

FOR PRIVATE CLIENTS

Inviting men and/or women of all ages ready for love

Are you ready for the language of love? Whether you are looking to flourish or find new, **SoulMateLove** is for you. This program experience enhances your chances as you receive **A Code of Love** identification system, and the means to discover and/or sustain your life partner. You can discover, develop, and attract life-long love and happiness into your life.

GLOSSARY - Gender Dynamics Intelligence Archetypes

RULER Masculine-Minded Male (MM)

Overview: The Ruler, embodying the Masculine-Minded Male (MM), epitomizes strength, decisiveness, and autonomy. He prioritizes logic and action over emotions, maintaining a commanding presence in various aspects of life.

Physical Characteristics: Physically, the Ruler typically boasts broad shoulders, a straight posture, and angular facial features. His demeanor exudes power and confidence.

Mental Attributes: Driven by logic and process-oriented thinking, the Ruler is decisive and assertive. However, he may become overly direct when under pressure, unwavering in his convictions.

Leadership Preferences: The Ruler expects clear answers and seeks control in all endeavors. He thrives in competitive environments, aiming for dominance and success.

Romantic Inclinations: In romantic relationships, the Ruler may struggle with emotional expression but excels in grand gestures of romance. Understanding his partner's emotional needs can pose a challenge.

Relationship Dynamics: Seeking a partner who appreciates his strength and leadership, the Ruler values compatibility and mutual respect. However, he may find difficulty with those who challenge his authority or fail to meet his expectations.

Guidance for the Ruler: Embrace flexibility and understanding in navigating romantic and professional interactions. Recognize the importance of emotional connection and be open to understanding your partner's perspective. Strive for balanced leadership that values assertiveness alongside empathy and collaboration.

NOTES:...
....
....
....
....
....
....
....
....

PHILOSOPHER Feminine-Minded Male (FM)

Overview: The Philosopher, embodying the Feminine-Minded Male (FM), represents sensitivity, intuition, and creativity. He values emotional connection and prefers a gentle approach to relationships and problem-solving.

Physical Characteristics: Physically, the FM typically possesses softer features, with a gentle shoulder line and facial structure. His body shape may lean towards a slighter frame, often wider at the hip line, reflecting his softer persona.

Mental Attributes: Driven by intuition and feelings, the Philosopher prioritizes deep thinking and interpersonal connections. He excels in verbal communication and values relationships over strict logic and rationality.

Leadership Preferences: The FM adopts a servant leadership style, focusing on understanding and meeting the emotional needs of those around him. He values collaboration and empathy in his interactions.

Romantic Inclinations: In romantic relationships, the Philosopher may struggle with traditional notions of masculinity but excels in emotional intimacy and thoughtful gestures. He appreciates deep conversations and values companionship over dominance.

Relationship Dynamics: Seeking a partner who appreciates his sensitivity and emotional intelligence, the Philosopher values mutual understanding and respect. He may find compatibility with individuals who embrace his gentle nature and value emotional connection.

Guidance for the Philosopher: Embrace your intuitive nature and prioritize emotional connection in both personal and professional interactions. Recognize the strength in your sensitivity and use it to build meaningful relationships. Challenge traditional stereotypes of masculinity and embrace your unique qualities as a source of strength and authenticity.

NOTES:..
....
....
....
....
....
....
....
....

MAGICIAN Masculine-Minded Female (MF)

Overview: The Magician, embodying the Masculine-Minded Female (MF), represents strength, assertiveness, and strategic thinking. She balances logic and emotion to navigate relationships and pursue her goals with determination.

Physical Characteristics: Physically, the MF often exhibits angular or straight bone structures, with broad or square shoulders and a straight stance. She carries herself with confidence and gravitates towards simple, no-fuss attire that reflects her pragmatic nature.

Mental Attributes: Driven by logic and process-oriented thinking, the Magician excels in spatial awareness and big-picture views. While she values emotions, she often relies on rationality and practicality to guide her decisions and actions.

Leadership Preferences: The MF adopts an assertive and collaborative leadership style, seeking consensus while prioritizing efficiency and effectiveness. She values teamwork and appreciates those who can match her strength and determination.

Romantic Inclinations: In romantic relationships, the Magician may struggle to express vulnerability but seeks a partner who appreciates her intellect and strength. She values companionship and respects her partner's ability to keep pace with her ambitious nature.

Relationship Dynamics: Seeking balance between her masculine and feminine energies, the MF values collaborative partnerships where her strengths are recognized and celebrated. She may appear intimidating at times but harbors deep feelings and desires authentic connection.

Guidance for the Magician: Embrace both your strength and vulnerability, recognizing that expressing emotions is not a sign of weakness but of authenticity. Seek partnerships that honor and value your intellect, strength, and determination, allowing you to thrive in both personal and professional endeavors. Strive for balance between your masculine and feminine energies, finding harmony in your relationships and personal growth.

NOTES:...
....
....
....
....
....
....
....

SOVEREIGN Feminine-Minded Female (FF)

Overview: The Sovereign, embodying the Feminine-Minded Female (FF), radiates nurturing energy and strength. She prioritizes relationships and seeks harmony and well-being for herself and those around her.

Physical Characteristics: Physically, the FF often possesses soft curves and gentle features, with a curved bust line and a longer waist. She carries herself with grace and prefers attire that accentuates her feminine qualities.

Mental Attributes: Driven by intuition and emotions, the Sovereign relies on her keen sense of empathy and verbal dexterity. She excels in nurturing relationships and attending to the finer details of life.

Leadership Preferences: The FF adopts a nurturing and protective leadership style, prioritizing the well-being of her community and those under her care. She values collaboration and compassion in her interactions.

Romantic Inclinations: In romantic relationships, the Sovereign seeks deep emotional connections and values partners who appreciate her nurturing nature. She may struggle with assertiveness at times but desires a partner who respects and supports her strengths.

Relationship Dynamics: Balancing strength and vulnerability, the FF values loyalty and compassion in her relationships. She may appear high-maintenance, yet harbors deep feelings and desires genuine connection.

Guidance for the Sovereign: Embrace your nurturing nature and recognize the strength in vulnerability. Seek partnerships that honor and value your compassion and empathy, allowing you to thrive in both personal and professional realms. Strive to find balance between assertiveness and sensitivity, embracing your feminine qualities as sources of power and authenticity. Seek partnerships that appreciate and complement your strengths, fostering mutual growth and harmony.

NOTES:...
....
....
....
....
....

FOR MORE INFORMATION

Contact dr.pauline@corporateheartinternational.com

www. corporateheartinternational.com

www.ingramcontent.com/pod-product-compliance
Lightning Source LLC
Chambersburg PA
CBHW071011120626
46546CB00003B/1041